English Medieval Armies
1066–1307
History, Organisation and Equipment

GABRIELE ESPOSITO

HISTORIC ARMIES SERIES, VOLUME 1

Title page image: Knight armed with sword and mace. (Milites Pagenses)

Contents page image: Knight of the early 12th century. (Les Seigneurs d'Orient)

Acknowledgements

This book is dedicated to my exceptional parents, Maria Rosaria and Benedetto. A very special thanks is due to Jonathan Jackson and Brianne Bellio of Key Publishing, for having believed in my editorial projects from the beginning and for their great intelligence. Their love for history and passion for publishing were fundamental for the birth of this present book. A very special mention goes to the brilliant re-enactment groups that allowed me access to their photos for the creation of this book: without the incredible work of research of their members, in fact, the final result of this publication would have not been the same. As a result, I want to express my deep gratitude to the following living history associations: Historia Aquitanorum, De Gueules et d'Argent, Milites Pagenses, Les Guerriers du Moyen-Age and Les Seigneurs d'Orient from France; Sericum et ferrum from Germany; Confraternita del Leone from Italy; Armin Kaar from Austria; and The Last Prince – O'Sullivan Beare from Ireland.

Published by Key Books
An imprint of Key Publishing Ltd
PO Box 100
Stamford
Lincs PE9 1XQ

www.keypublishing.com

The right of Gabriele Esposito to be identified as the author of this book has been asserted in accordance with the Copyright, Designs and Patents Act 1988 Sections 77 and 78.

Copyright © Gabriele Esposito, 2023

ISBN 978 1 80282 588 6

All rights reserved. Reproduction in whole or in part in any form whatsoever or by any means is strictly prohibited without the prior permission of the Publisher.

Typeset by SJmagic DESIGN SERVICES, India.

Contents

Introduction		4
Chapter 1	The Norman Conquest of England	6
Chapter 2	The Reign of William the Conqueror: 1066–1087	16
Chapter 3	The Reigns of William II and Henry I: 1087–1135	23
Chapter 4	The Anarchy: 1135–1154	31
Chapter 5	The Reign of Henry II: 1154–1189	47
Chapter 6	The Reign of Richard the Lionheart: 1189–1199	64
Chapter 7	The Reign of King John: 1199–1216	70
Chapter 8	The Reign of Henry III: 1216–1272	83
Chapter 9	The Reign of Edward I: 1272–1307	94
Chapter 10	Military Organisation and Equipment in the Medieval British Isles	104
Bibliography		124
The Re-enactors who Contributed to this Book		125

Introduction

After the Norman Conquest of 1066, the English lands gradually lost their Saxon character and became much more similar to continental Europe; feudalism was brought to the British Isles by the Normans, together with a new model of centralised monarchy, thus changing the administrative and social structures of England forever. The Normans were, without a doubt, some of the most effective military fighters of the Middle Ages, who, thanks to their great martial capabilities, were able to win two major realms for themselves – one in England and one in Southern Italy – during a turbulent historical period that was characterised by great political fragmentation for Europe. They are generally considered as the perfect representation of the iconic feudal knight, a professional soldier equipped with full armour and fighting as a heavy cavalryman. It should be remembered, however, that the feudal military system based on the prominence of armoured cavalry was not created by the Normans: it was introduced by Charlemagne (2 April 747–28 January 814) and by his Carolingian successors, but it was the Normans who interpreted and formalised it in the most effective way.

If compared to all the other fighters of their age, the Normans had a somewhat different nature due to their peculiar ethnic origins. They were the direct heirs of the Viking raiders who settled in northern France during the 10th century and gave their name to the region known today as 'Normandy'. The Normans always retained the impressive military 'furor' (fury) of their Scandinavian ancestors, but soon transformed themselves from pirates to feudal warlords. They became the most powerful vassals of the King of France and adopted the feudal military institutions in full, learning from their former enemies. The Normans transformed themselves from foot warriors armed with axes to heavily armoured knights trained to charge in close order with spear and shield. The feudal knights of France were no match for them, and thus Norman leaders started to play a prominent role in the politics of the French realm. The Norman knights or 'milites' had the best military equipment of their age: nasal helmet, chainmail, kite shield and long sword. They rode the best horses in continental Europe and learned how to fight on horseback during their childhood. Thanks to the use of stirrups and saddles with tall pommels, a Norman knight could enjoy a high degree of stability while fighting on horseback and could charge with his spear tucked under his armpit: this enabled him to hit his targets with all the great kinetic speed derived from his horse's run. Any enemy infantryman, armoured or not, could not withstand the charge of the Norman milites; the latter usually attacked in small tactical groups of 20–25 knights, known as 'conrois', which were deployed on the battlefield in wedge formation. Thanks to their military superiority, the Normans started to expand their territorial domains in northern France and were employed as mercenaries across the Mediterranean.

In this book, we will cover the history, organisation and equipment of the English armies that fought the many wars between 1066 and 1307. We will follow the Normans through their incredible campaigns of conquest, which had enormous success, and see how the most famous Duke of Normandy, William the Conqueror (c.1028–9 September 1087), invaded the Kingdom of England in 1066 and progressively transformed it into the most important Norman realm in Europe. After a few decades, however, the new royal family initiated by William the Conqueror disappeared due to the lack of direct heirs, and thus the Kingdom of England entered a chaotic phase characterised by civil conflicts as well as by the search for a new royal house that could assume control over the turbulent lands. This historical period, known as 'The Anarchy', began in 1135 and ended only in 1154 when the first Plantagenet, Henry II (5 March

1133–6 July 1189), was crowned as monarch of the English realm. The new royal family would keep power over its kingdom for more than three centuries, until the outbreak of the War of the Roses (1455–1487). During this long period, the Plantagenet kings fought a series of conflicts, which can be grouped into three main categories: wars fought against the French monarchy in continental Europe; wars fought in the British Isles against the 'Celtic nations' (Wales, Scotland and Ireland); and civil conflicts fought in England against rebel aristocrats. Sometimes, wars belonging to two different categories could take place at the same time: it was not uncommon, in fact, to see the English nobles rebelling against their king while the latter was campaigning on the borders of the realm or in France. The historical period covered in this book ends with the year 1307, which saw the death of Edward I (17/18 June 1239–7 July 1307), one of the greatest Plantagenet monarchs). In the first two centuries of their rule over England, the Plantagenets created an expansionist dynasty: their main political objective was that of conquering a large portion of the British Isles by defeating the political entities that bordered England. By the end of the period covered in this book, they had reached their ambitious objectives only partially: Wales had been conquered thanks to the military efforts of Edward I, while most of Ireland and the whole of Scotland remained fully independent. This situation would remain more or less unchanged well after the end of the Hundred Years' War (1337–1453), showing that the defeat of the Celtic nations was not as easy to achieve as the Plantagenets had initially expected. In this book, special attention will be given to the wars fought by England against Wales, Scotland and Ireland; at the same time, it will provide a detailed overview of the 'minor' conflicts that saw the Plantagenet monarchs campaigning in France. These were just a precursor to the longer war that would start in 1337, but still had significant consequences for the history of England. Richard the Lionheart (8 September 1157–6 April 1199), the most famous of the Plantagenet kings, was killed while besieging a castle in France, and his infamous brother, John (24 December 1166–19 October 1216), was forced to sign the famous Magna Carta, mostly due to the defeat that he had suffered at the hands of the French during the Battle of Bouvines (27 July 1214), one of the largest pitched clashes fought during the age of feudal Europe. Like their Norman predecessors, the Plantagenets were French aristocrats before becoming monarchs of England; as a result, they always retained large territorial possessions in continental Europe and remained – from a formal point of view – vassals of the King of France. It is clear, however, that a king being the vassal of another king was very difficult in practice, and this caused most of the Anglo-French conflicts covered in this work. The most brutal wars of the early Plantagenet period, however, were without a doubt the civil conflicts fought against the rebellious nobles; since the beginning, in fact, the concept of 'centralised monarchy' was met with great resistance from the English aristocrats.

Chapter 1
The Norman Conquest of England

On 5 January 1066, the Saxon King of England, Edward the Confessor (born c.1003) died without direct heirs; this caused the beginning of the worst dynastical crisis ever seen in England during the central Middle Ages. Four different 'pretenders' claimed their right to sit on the English throne: the first was Edgar Ætheling (c.1052–c.1125), who was just 15 in 1066 and the grandson of Edmund Ironside (c.990–30 November 1016), who had been King of England for a few months during 1016; the second was Harold Godwinson (c.1022–14 October 1066), Earl of Wessex, who was Edward the Confessor's brother-in-law but who had no blood connection with the defunct king; the third was Harald Hardrada (c.1015–25 September 1066), Viking King of Norway since 1046, who had no blood ties with Edward the Confessor; the fourth was William, Duke of Normandy since 1035, who was a cousin of the defunct king through Edward's mother Emma (who was William's great-aunt). Edward the Confessor had promised his throne to both William and Harold during two different phases of his long life, and this caused great confusion. The weakest of the pretenders was Edgar Ætheling, who was the only one who could not count on an army to support his claims. Harald Hardrada was a true Viking and had strong military forces, but his claims on the English throne were weak from a dynastic point of view. Despite this, he decided to invest England after concluding an important alliance with Tostig Godwinson (c.1029–25 September 1066), who revolted against his brother Harold Godwinson after the latter was proclaimed King of England in 1066 by the Saxon aristocracy. After Edward the Confessor's death, the Saxon nobles elected Harold as their king very rapidly, in an attempt to protect themselves from the possibility of being ruled by a foreigner, and gain the upper hand in upcoming military events, as they had correctly predicted that both Norman and Viking armies would soon be attacking. Therefore, while to some Harald Hardrada's landing on English shores would have been perceived as just another Viking invasion, the Norwegian warlord had good chances of victory, as Harold Godwinson would soon be obliged to divide his military forces into two parts.

After hearing of Harold Godwinson's coronation, William of Normandy started assembling a massive fleet in order to transport his military forces to England. He could count on the support of the English Church and any nobles who were against Harold's political plans. The new Saxon king prepared himself to face the Normans and recruited a very large army that comprised a significant number of professional warriors. The Saxons deployed themselves to the Isle of Wight and waited for the arrival of the Normans. The latter, however, were blocked in their ports for seven months due to unfavourable weather conditions, and thus William could not conduct his invasion with the planned timing. This delay also caused significant problems for Harold, as his plan had to defeat the Normans before facing the second invasion led by Harald Hardrada. The Saxon king knew that the Vikings would need some months to assemble a sizeable invasion force, as opposed to the Normans, who could be ready and able to attack in just a few weeks. The delay of seven months suffered by William meant that the two invasions would take place exactly in the same time frame. Harold knew that the Normans would plan to land in Southern England, and theorised that Harald Hardrada's target would be East Anglia or Northumbria. The Vikings, coming from Norway, landed on 8 September 1066, at the mouth of the River Tyne with Northumbria as their first target. As mentioned above, Harald Hardrada counted on the support of Tostig Godwinson, who had revolted against his brother Harold and had already tried to form an alliance with William of Normandy. When the latter refused his offer, Tostig went to the King of Norway and decided to join him in his invasion of England. The brother of the Saxon monarch proved to be a precious ally for Harald Hardrada, since he was well acquainted with the terrain on which the Vikings were going to operate, and also because he was in contact with several of the most important Saxon nobles of northern England. After joining his forces with those of Tostig, Harald sailed along the River Ouse towards the city of York. The city had once been the most important stronghold of the Vikings in England, and thus its recapture would have been very important for the Scandinavian invasion forces. Harold Godwinson had entrusted the defence of the northern part of his kingdom to the two most powerful warlords of the area: Edwin (died 1071), Earl of Mercia, and Morcar (died c.1087), Earl of Northumbria, who were brothers. The brothers had already mobilised part of their military forces in view of the Viking invasion and thus were able to quickly move against Harald in order to prevent the fall of York. On 20 September, not far from the city, they fought against the Scandinavians at the Battle of Fulford. The Vikings were 10,000 in total, while

Knight equipped with sword and kite shield. (Historia Aquitanorum)

the Saxons were in clear numerical inferiority with just 4,500 warriors (3,000 from Northumbria and 1,500 from Mercia). Edwin and Morcar, however, could deploy their forces in a strong defensive position that had the River Ouse on the right flank and a swampy area known as the 'Fordland' on the left. Harald deployed his forces on higher ground, but could not conduct any manoeuvre of encirclement on the wings of his enemy. However, at the beginning of the clash, the Saxons made a great mistake: instead of remaining in their defensive positions, they decided to launch a frontal attack against the Vikings. The Saxon offensive took place while the Scandinavians were still completing the deployment of their troops, but the result was a complete failure; Harald soon organised a counter-attack with his best warriors and forced the Saxons to give ground. The decisive moment of the battle came when, against all odds, the Vikings were able cross the River Ouse on one side and the Fordland on the other. Outnumbered and outmanoeuvred, the warriors of Edwin

Knight wearing a padded 'aketon' (a padded defensive jacket) under his 'hauberk' (military tunic) of chainmail. (Historia Aquitanorum)

and Morcar had no choice but to flee from the battlefield. York was occupied by the Vikings soon after this victory, and it became clear that northern England was now open to Harald Hardrada's conquest. When news of the Fulford defeat reached Harold Godwinson, the Saxon monarch was shocked but reacted rapidly, force-marching his royal army 190 miles north from London to York in order to prevent the raiding of the northern part of his kingdom. Harold was known to be a great military leader, and this was confirmed by the fact that, within a week of the Battle of Fulford, his forces were already facing Harald Hardrada at York.

Knight from the 11th century. In the background, there is a trebuchet, one of the many siege weapons employed by the Normans. (Les Seigneurs d'Orient)

The Saxon warriors who arrived in the northern theatre of operations were extremely tired, since they had marched day and night for a week; they, however, were more numerous than their opponents. According to modern estimates, the Vikings had lost 1,000 men at the Battle of Fulford, and thus were 9,000 in total. Harold, by contrast, had mustered 10,000 infantrymen and 2,000 cavalrymen. The Scandinavians were taken by surprise, having not envisaged that the Saxon royal army could reach York in such a brief time. The decisive clash of Harald Hardrada's invasion of England took place at Stamford Bridge, on the River Derwent. When the battle began, some Viking forces were on the western bank of the river, while the majority were on the eastern bank, since they were unaware that the Saxons were moving towards their positions. Caught by surprise, the Scandinavians on the eastern bank of the Derwent decided to deploy themselves in a defensive 'circle' formation. Those on the western bank were rapidly massacred by the Saxons, and just a few of them were able to escape by crossing the bridge that gave the battle its name. However, while seemingly in a strong position, Harold had to face a serious problem; his troops had no choice but to pass through the chokepoint represented by the bridge in order to attack the Vikings. According to contemporary sources, a single giant warrior from the army of Harald Hardrada (armed with a massive two-handed axe) blocked the narrow crossing and repulsed the Saxon warriors alone for some time. He killed 40 enemies before a Saxon warrior floated under the bridge and thrust his spear through the planks in order to mortally wound the giant axeman. After pouring onto the eastern bank of the Derwent, the Saxons deployed themselves in battle line just short of the Viking circle, locked their shields and charged against the defensive formation of the enemy. The ensuing phase of the battle, characterised by harsh hand-to-hand fighting, lasted for hours and saw the Scandinavians resisting with great determination. Both sides suffered heavy losses, and the outcome of the clash was unpredictable until the end. Harald Hardrada fought with great courage among his elite warriors and withstood the assault for as long as possible; at a certain point, however, the defensive formation of the Viking army began to fragment, and the initial cohesion was lost. The Saxons were finally able to break the enemy's 'wall of shields' and gradually started to surround isolated groups of Scandinavians. When it became clear that his army was in the process of being outflanked, Harald Hardrada did not attempt to abandon the battlefield but instead continued to fight at the head of his remaining warriors. He was killed by an enemy arrow, after which his troops went into a state of complete chaos. During this final phase of the clash, Tostig Godwinson was also killed. When everything was seemingly lost for the Scandinavians, some Viking reinforcements arrived on the battlefield; these consisted of warriors who had been left behind by Harald in order to guard his warships and who were under the command of his prospective son-in-law, Eystein Orre. Eystein launched a violent counter-attack against the Saxons, which was easily repulsed by Harold's men, and Eystein was killed during the fight. After several hours of intense combat, Harald Hardrada's impressive Viking army had been completely wiped out. According to contemporary sources, so many Saxons and Norwegians died at Stamford Bridge that the battlefield upon which the clash took place was still whitened with bleached bones 50 years later. After obtaining such a brilliant victory, Harold Godwinson concluded a truce with the surviving Vikings, and they were allowed to leave England after giving pledges not to attack the Saxon Kingdom again. The losses of the Scandinavians were so severe that just 24 of their 300 warships returned back to Norway. Harold had destroyed the military forces of one of his rivals, but the losses of his army had been substantial ones.

Just three days after the Battle of Stamford Bridge, on 28 September, William and his Normans landed in Southern England on Pevensey Bay, Sussex. Without having the time to replenish his losses and to reorganise his troops, Harold had to march south rapidly at the head of his exhausted warriors. After defeating the Vikings in the north, Harold left some of his troops in Northern England under the control of Morcar and Edwin in order to prevent any further Norwegian attacks. He, with the best elements of his army, marched south very rapidly and stopped for just a few days in London. It is likely that the Saxon troops spent about a week on their march south, averaging about 27 miles per day; this was something absolutely incredible for the standards of the time. For the second time in a few days, the Saxon military forces covered an immense distance, and when they arrived in the south to intercept the Normans, they were tired but their morale was extremely high.

We cannot know what could have happened if the Saxons had faced the Normans before meeting Harald Hardrada's army, but Harold made a great strategic mistake when he decided to leave the southern territories of his kingdom to stop the invasion of Northumbria. The Vikings needed several weeks to reach the heartland of the Saxon territories in the south, and could have been slowed down in their advance by some local forces. The Battle of Hastings, fought by the troops of Harold Godwinson and William the Conqueror on 14 October 1066, is one of the most iconic moments in the military history of the British Isles, and it shaped the destiny of England for the centuries to come. The exact numbers and composition of the Norman invasion force are unknown, but, thanks to some details that can be found in different primary sources, it is possible to provide an approximate 'order of battle' of William's troops. The Normans were 13,000 in total, consisting of 10,000 infantrymen and 3,000 cavalrymen. The foot soldiers were mostly equipped with helmets and chainmail, as were the mounted milites; a certain number of the infantrymen, however, consisted of 'missile troops' (archers and crossbowmen). Most of the mounted soldiers were professional fighters coming from the northern regions of France, but they also included a certain number of lightly equipped mounted squires (servants) who assisted the milites as auxiliaries. The missile troops, also numbering around 3,000 men, played one of the most important roles during the clash. The standard equipment of the Norman soldiers was quite heavy, since it comprised helmet with nasal and chainmail 'hauberk', which was, in most cases, knee-length and long-sleeved. All cavalrymen and infantrymen, except for the mounted servants and missile troops, carried a shield made of wood that was reinforced on the external edges with a strip of metal. This was kite-shaped for most of the cavalrymen and infantrymen, but some of the latter used round shields similar to the Saxon ones. The main weapon of the Norman

Knight equipped with hauberk of chainmail. (Sericum et ferrum)

knights, in addition to the long sword, was the couched lance, which was carried tucked against the body under the right arm. The infantrymen had a longer spear that was used like a sort of pike, while missile troops wore no armour except for a simple conical helmet. The Saxon military forces also consisted of around 12,000–13,000 soldiers but had a different internal composition. Besides a few archers, Harold's forces did not comprise sizeable contingents of cavalry or missile troops, rather, the Saxon army that fought at Hastings was a compact infantry force. Three thousand of the Saxon warriors were elite 'housecarls' (professional fighters in royal service), while the remaining 10,000 were 'thegns' (professionals, but inferior to the housecarls) or 'fyrdmen' (non-professional fighters). The thegns came from several different areas of England, since they had been mobilised by Harold to face the Scandinavian invasion of Harald Hardrada, while the fyrdmen mostly came from the regions of Southern England that were exposed to the Norman invasion.

On the night of 13 October, Harold and his men camped at Caldbec Hill and started to prepare themselves for the upcoming battle. The Saxon monarch did not have precise information about the composition of William's forces, but wanted to intercept them before they could move further inland.

Above left: Knight equipped with nasal helmet. (Historia Aquitanorum)

Above right: Knight armed with sword and mace. (Milites Pagenses)

It was the Normans, however, who advanced for first. Harold established a very strong defensive position at the top of Caldbec Hill and deployed his men in a massive shield wall. On the back of the ordinary infantrymen, the 'housecarls' were used as a strategic reserve, along with the few missile troops. Launching a frontal attack against the Saxon positions on Caldbec Hill would have been extremely difficult for the Normans, who would likely have suffered severe losses during their advance from missiles thrown by the enemy, and who were also extremely tired after having marched for many days and thus were in no condition to launch a massive attack. With this in mind, Harold decided to fight a defensive battle. The fight took place at the present-day town of Battle, in East Sussex, which is located between Caldbec Hill to the north and Telham Hill to the south. Harold's forces were deployed in a small-but-dense formation at the top of a steep slope, with their flanks protected by woods and with some marshy ground in front of them. William arranged his troops in three groups, also known as 'battles', which were assembled according to the geographical provenience of the various soldiers. The left battle consisted of soldiers coming from Brittany, Anjou, Poitou and Maine; all being under the control of the Duchy of Normandy and the most strategically important of them being Brittany. The central battle consisted of the army's strongest soldiers, coming from Normandy and commanded by William. The right battle consisted of soldiers coming from Picardy, Boulogne and Flanders; this group included a good number of mercenaries, and thus its members were not feudal levies but professional soldiers. The front lines of each battle were made up of archers and a few crossbowmen; the infantrymen were deployed on the back of the missile troops and the cavalry was held in reserve. William wanted to open the battle with his excellent archers, in order to weaken the strong defensive positions of Harold with a 'rain of arrows'. His plan was to order an infantry charge after the end of his light troops' attacks; the foot soldiers were then to create some openings in the Saxon ranks to be exploited by a final cavalry charge, which would have decided the outcome of the battle. The Normans attacked first, but since the beginning of the clash it was clear that William's plan was not going to work: the archers started shooting uphill at the Saxon shield wall but to very little effect. The uphill angle at which they were firing meant that the arrows either bounced on the enemy shields or overshot their targets. Having understood that his missile troops were of little use, William ordered his infantry to attack. The Norman foot soldiers, however, were met with a barrage of missiles (including axes and stones in addition to arrows) and thus were unable to open any gap in the enemy's shield wall. The cavalry joined the infantry in the attack, but most of the Norman milites were not able to even reach the top of the hill due to their heavy personal equipment. At this point, a rumour started that William had been killed; this caused great confusion among the Normans, who were already retreating. The Saxons began attacking the retreating invaders with the objective of routing them, but William rode through his forces showing his face and yelling that he was still alive. With renewed vigour, a Norman counter-attack was organised, which stopped the Saxon offensive and caused a temporary break in the fighting. The Saxon attack repulsed by the Normans had not been ordered by Harold and thus had been spontaneous: the Saxon monarch, in fact, did not want to abandon his strong defensive positions. During the lull in the fighting, which probably occurred in the early afternoon, the opposing sides had a break for rest and food. William, meanwhile, constructed a new battle plan that was inspired by the events of the morning, and understanding that the Saxons could become extremely vulnerable if they abandoned their positions on top of the hill. On the plain, the Norman cavalrymen could charge against the Saxon infantrymen and cause severe losses.

When fighting resumed, William sent his cavalry against the Saxons two times; the Normans attacked for a few minutes but soon made a feigned flight after their advance, in the hope of inducing the enemy to move down from the hill and launch a counter-attack. Several Saxon soldiers abandoned their positions and followed the retreating Norman horsemen in close pursuit; by abandoning the wall of shields that

Above left: Knight with nasal helmet and kite shield. (Historia Aquitanorum)

Above right: Knight equipped with nasal helmet and triangular shield; the latter evolved from the previous kite shield. (De Gueules et d'Argent)

had been deployed by Harold, however, they became an easy target for the enemy missile troops. Once on the plain, the Saxons were stopped by the enemy infantry and were charged by the Norman cavalrymen who ended their feigned retreat. Being on the open field and having no time to deploy themselves in a defensive formation, the Saxon warriors were massacred by the Norman milites, who launched several deadly charges. Harold, who had not been able to keep discipline among the ranks of his army, was killed during this chaotic phase of the clash while he was trying to stop his men. The Saxon king died from an arrow to the eye; his sudden death left the Saxon troops leaderless in the most delicate moment of the

Knights wearing two different variations of the famous nasal helmet. (Historia Aquitanorum)

struggle. Most of the thegns and fyrdmen had abandoned their positions on the top of the hill and thus were progressively routed by the Normans on the plain. In contrast, most of the housecarls retained their usual discipline and remained on top of the hill with the firm intention of defending the body of their monarch. Here they continued to fight until the end, until the last one of them was killed by the enemy (who now had an enormous numerical superiority). With the death of Harold and of his formidable housecarls at Hastings, William of Normandy became 'the Conqueror' and the history of the British Isles changed forever. The history of Norman England had begun.

Chapter 2

The Reign of William the Conqueror 1066–1087

After crushing the Saxon royal army at Hastings, William hoped that the conquest of his new realm would be completed quite rapidly. The Saxon nobles and clergy, however, decided to not surrender; they nominated Edgar Ætheling – son of Edmund Ironside – as their king and organised their resistance against the Norman invaders. William's first moves in England were quite intelligent: he secured Dover – transforming it into his main naval base from which supplies and reinforcements could come from Normandy – and the important religious centre of Canterbury. He then sent a token force to occupy Winchester, where the Saxon royal treasury was preserved. In late November of 1066, he entered London, without facing any serious opposition. After crossing the Thames River, William came to control most of Southern England; as a result, several of the Saxon aristocrats who had decided to resist after Hastings – including Edgar Ætheling – submitted to the Norman ruler without fighting. On Christmas Day, William was crowned King of England at Westminster Abbey. The new monarch, knowing very well that in northern England the local communities resented his rule, tried to form a solid alliance with those Saxon northern nobles who had joined his cause by confirming them in their lands and titles. Moreover, various bishops were all confirmed, since William was well aware of the great power that the Church had in England. Soon after assuming power in his new kingdom, William went back to Normandy for a few months in order to stabilise his political position in northern France, as one of his former local allies, Eustace II of Boulogne (c.1015–c.1087), was revolting against him. While the Norman king was absent, the Saxons reorganised themselves in northern England under the guidance of Harold Godwinson's mother, Gytha. She had the centre of her power in the city of Exeter, where the Saxon resistance gathered a good portion of its military forces. In December 1067, William the Conqueror returned to England and besieged Exeter, which was conquered by the Normans after a short siege. Meanwhile, some other relatives of Harold, including his sons, landed near Bristol with the objective of

**Knight wearing a nasal helmet.
(Les Seigneurs d'Orient)**

Knight of the 11th century. The early heraldic designs painted on kite shields, like the one shown here, were quite simple. (Historia Aquitanorum)

launching a major revolt but were defeated by the local Norman forces. In 1068, the Saxon warlords Edwin and Morcar, who had temporarily supported William after the Saxon defeat at Hastings, also revolted against the Normans.

The uprising of two of the most influential Saxon nobles represented a serious problem for King William, who soon understood that the only way to assume effective control over his entire realm was to defeat the Saxon aristocrats and to replace them with loyal Norman nobles. Feudalism, which was well-established in Normandy, did not exist in England; as a result, a new nobility made up of landowners had to be created almost from zero. In addition, the Normans also had to build a new network of castles across England, with which they could control the territory in an effective way. Such fortifications would be assigned to the new nobles coming from Normandy and defended by substantial garrisons. The period that started after the uprising of Edwin and Morcar was characterised by a series of devastating military campaigns conducted in northern England, and saw the Normans employing very harsh repressive methods in order to end any form of Saxon resistance. It was the so-called 'Harrying of the North', one of the most controversial pages in the personal history of William the Conqueror. In the summer of 1068, William invaded Northumbria and occupied the city of York; soon after the main Norman army left the urban centre, however, the garrison left behind by the king was besieged by the Saxons. William was forced to come back to Northumbria and to defeat the local rebels again, while minor Saxon uprisings broke out practically in every corner of his realm. By now, Edgar Ætheling had changed sides and was at war with the Normans; the Saxon leader, however, knew very well that without some help coming from abroad, he would not be able to defeat the invaders. As a result, Edgar made an alliance with Sweyn II (c. 1019–28 April 1076), the King of Denmark and a nephew of Cnut the Great (died 12 November 1035).

Sweyn assembled a large fleet and sent it – under the control of his sons – to the coast of Northumbria. The Danes raided the eastern coastline of England before conquering York and joining forces with the Saxon insurgents. The new menace was a particularly serious one, since the Scandinavian warriors who were now on English soil were professional fighters. In the winter of 1069, King William marched with his royal army from Nottingham to York, with the objective of fighting a pitched battle against his enemies; when he reached the Northumbrian city, however, the Danes had already moved with all their ships to the Humber Estuary. After these events, some negotiations took place between William and the Danish leaders, and in the end the king agreed to pay a large sum of money to the Scandinavians in exchange for their promise of leaving England immediately and without fighting. At this point, after the Danes disappeared, William turned his attention to the Saxon rebels. He and his men acted in a very cruel way: many villages were burned to ashes, crops and herds were confiscated, hundreds of civilians were killed without reason, and the reserves of food of the local communities were destroyed. These acts caused the death of over 100,000 people, most of whom died of starvation. William was using 'psychological warfare' to terrorise his enemies and to eradicate any form of Saxon resistance from Northern England. The Normans' acts of devastation were accompanied by the building of several new castles, most of which were – at least initially – only small fortifications made of wood and not massive stone ones. One after the other, all the rebel Saxon aristocrats surrendered and Norman castles were built in Nottingham, York, Lincoln, Huntingdon, Cambridge, Chester and Stafford. By April 1070, William the Conqueror had completely pacified the northern part of his kingdom and thus could work to create a strong alliance with the English clergy. His conquest of the realm was officially recognised by the Pope, who sent three of his legates to Winchester to crown William again in a new ceremony. In exchange for this important religious investiture, the Norman monarch agreed to replace several Saxon bishops and abbots with new French ones who could be controlled more directly by the Pope.

Above left: Knight of the 11th century. The kind of helmet shown in this reconstruction was quite common in Continental Europe. (Sericum et ferrum)

Above right: Knight armed with mace; note the practice of wearing chainmail only on the leg that was not protected by the shield. (De Gueules et d'Argent)

King William, however, still had to face some threats to the stability of his kingdom coming from abroad. In the spring of 1070, Sweyn of Denmark attacked England again with a large fleet. The Scandinavian monarch joined forces with some local Saxon insurgents, but after several weeks of campaigning, he was able to achieve very little – except for looting some religious buildings – and thus returned back home. During 1071, William fought again against his main Saxon enemies: Edwin and Morcar. The first was betrayed by his own men and killed, while the second went to the Isle of Ely where he tried to resist. The Normans landed on the island, defeated Morcar and captured him. In 1072, William had to face a new foreign invasion, this time coming from the northern borders of his realm. King Malcolm III of Scotland (died 13 November 1093) invaded Northern England in the hope of gaining some border territories thanks to the internal troubles experienced by the Normans. William defeated Malcolm easily after a brief campaign and concluded a peace treaty with him; as part of this, Edgar Ætheling, who had sought refuge in Malcolm's court, was expelled from Scotland. During 1073, King William had to leave England for Normandy, as his continental possession of Maine was attacked by the Count of Anjou. After a few weeks of fighting, the Norman monarch was able to prevail, but the general strategic situation of his French domains was worsening.

The Count of Anjou and the Count of Flanders were strongly determined to limit Norman power in northern France; to achieve their objectives, they could count on the decisive support of King Philip I of France, who feared that William the Conqueror could become much more powerful than him. In 1075, two of the major Norman nobles who had received land and properties in England – Ralph de Gael (before 1042–c.1100), Earl of Norfolk, and Roger de Breteuil (1056–after 1087), Earl of Hereford – organised a plot with the objective of overthrowing William. This, known as 'Revolt of the Earls', was sponsored and supported by the King of France. William was absent when the rebellion began, but his loyal vassals were able to crush the revolt alone and quite rapidly. The insurgents had invited a Danish fleet of 200 warships to England, but this arrived too late.

Soon after these events, William had to face an invasion of his Norman domains by King Philip I (23 May 1052–29 July 1108) of France; the latter, by 1076, was strongly determined to reduce the territorial extension and political power of the Duchy of Normandy. During this new war, for the first time in his long military career, William the Conqueror was defeated on the open field at the Battle of Dol. Despite this temporary setback, however, the Normans defeated the enemy forces that later tried to invest Maine. During 1077, the hostilities between William and Philip temporarily came to an end, but the King of England started to experience some serious troubles inside his own family. Robert (c.1051–February 1134), the eldest son of William, quarrelled with his younger brothers William (c.1056–2 August 1100) and Henry (c.1068–1 December 1135) over the succession of their father. Now that the ruling Duke of Normandy was also King of England, would his successor continue to control both territories or would they be divided? Would the eldest son have been given Normandy or England? In 1078, Robert, who wanted to receive Normandy before the death of his father, rebelled against William. He was given decisive support by King Philip, who assigned him the castle of Gerberoi on the border of Normandy. King William besieged his son and the rebels at Gerberoi; during the siege, a pitched battle took place between the two opposing sides and in this clash the old William was unhorsed by Robert. The king was saved by one of his English soldiers but was defeated and had to abandon the siege of Gerberoi. In 1080, father and son finally found a compromise, according to which the Duchy of Normandy was promised to Robert. Robert was more interested in becoming Duke of Normandy than receiving the English Crown; Normandy, after all, was richer than England at that time and many Norman nobles still considered William's conquest of England only as a 'temporary addition' to the Norman domains. While King William was campaigning in Normandy against Robert, King Malcolm of Scotland invaded northern England and raided the area located between the rivers Tweed and Tees. Encouraged by the foreign attack, the Northumbrians also rebelled against the Normans. William responded by sending his son Robert against the Scots, at the head of the royal army. Malcolm was defeated together with the Northumbrian rebels, and the Normans built new fortifications to defend the border of northern England. During 1083, Robert rebelled again against his father and renewed his alliance with the King of France; as a result, William went back to Normandy, where he had to fight in Maine to crush a local feudal revolt. The last years of William's long reign remained troubled, and during this time he fought against King Philip in Vexin. In July 1087, while burning the city of Mantes in Vexin, William suffered a fatal injury (probably caused by the pommel of his saddle). Before dying, William the Conqueror assigned the Duchy of Normandy to his first son Robert and gave custody of the Kingdom of England to his second son, William. Henry, his younger son, did not inherit any territories but rather a large sum of money. William, soon after the death of his father, was crowned King of England as William II.

William the Conqueror was a capable military leader but also an excellent administrator. He created a network of fortifications in England that was undeniably impressive, made up of castles but also of keeps and mottes. The Tower of London was also erected during his reign. William introduced feudalism in his new realm, assigning landed properties to his most loyal nobles who – in turn – gave fiefdoms to the knights at their service (this was the so-called 'sub-infeudation' system). Each of the Norman earls was to provide a fixed quota of knights to the king, not only for war service but also for providing garrisons to the various castles in times of peace. William was well known for his love of hunting and introduced the so-called 'forest law' in several areas of England, which dictated that only authorised individuals could hunt on the territory of the royal forests.

The Norman monarch never attempted to integrate Normandy and England into one unified political entity and thus – only for his French domains – he always remained

Knight of the 11th century. (Sericum et ferrum)

a vassal of the French monarchy. William chose not to reform the Saxon administrative system based on shires; as a result, the royal authority continued to be represented in each shire by public officials called 'sheriffs'. The king spent most of his rule travelling across his domains, in order to control the various territories in a direct way. Initially, he had very little knowledge of his new subjects' economic capabilities and of his new realm's resources. William, however, continued the collection of the Saxon 'danegeld' or 'land tax', which was an annual tax based on the value of landholdings and could be collected at differing rates (usually two shillings per hide in normal years, but which increased to six shillings in years of crisis). William enlarged the royal territorial possessions in England by absorbing the lands previously owned by Harold Godwinson, making him the largest secular landowner of the kingdom by a wide margin. At Christmas 1085, William the Conqueror ordered the compilation of a survey of the landholdings held by himself and his vassals throughout the Kingdom of England; he also decided to divide the territory of his realm into counties. The compilation resulted in a very important survey known as the 'Domesday Book', which consisted of a listing, made on a county basis, of the holdings of each landholder. The document described each holding in great detail, providing its value and tax assessment as well as other info (the number of peasants living on it, the number of ploughs that the locals had and the location of any significant natural or material resource). The 'Domesday Book', completed during 1086, is the most impressive record of feudal obligations ever produced during the Middle Ages and a perfect representation of William the Conqueror's great administrative capabilities.

Knights bearing kite shields. (Historia Aquitanorum)

Chapter 3
The Reigns of William II and Henry I
1087–1135

King William II, also known as 'William Rufus' or 'William the Red' because of the colour of his hair, had to face a series of political problems soon after becoming monarch of England. Many of the Norman nobles held landed properties on both sides of the Channel and had always been vassals of a single overlord, William the Conqueror; now that William was dead, these aristocrats were to become vassals of William II for their English possessions, and vassals of Robert – nicknamed 'Robert Curthose' or 'Robert Short Stockings' by his father – for their French possessions. Being the vassal of two lords who were probably going to fight against each other in the near future was not easy to sustain in the long term, and thus several Norman aristocrats were favourable to the idea of re-uniting England and Normandy under the guidance of a single monarch. Robert was considered as more expert and more ambitious than his younger brother and thus, in 1088, several of the major Norman feudal lords living in England organised a revolt against their new king. This rebellion was led by Bishop Odo of Bayeux (died 1097), half-brother of William the Conqueror, who had been deprived of most of his personal power during the latter's late reign. The rebel nobles planned their insurrection quite well, taking control of some key castles and stocking up on large amounts of provisions; William II's response to their actions, however, was very rapid and effective. As a first move, the young king promised those warlords who decided to fight on his side that they would receive as much money and land as they wanted. He then tried to win the favour of the English commoners, by promising them that he would promulgate new and fairer taxation and labour laws. Both moves worked: several aristocrats who had initially joined the revolt changed their minds and remained loyal to the legitimate king, while most of the common people started to consider the new monarch as someone who could improve their living conditions. The royal military forces, thanks to their numerical superiority, were thus able to crush the rebellion rapidly. Odo was besieged in Pevensey Castle and captured when his stronghold fell. Robert Curthose, uncertain about the outcome of the events, never left Normandy to disembark in England and failed to send the troops he had assembled to join Odo in time. After the end of the hostilities, William II was officially recognised as the legitimate King of England by his brother Robert.

However, in 1091, the hostilities between William II and Robert resumed, when the King of England attempted to invade the Duchy of Normandy. The new conflict, however, ended quickly and without any significant modification to the status quo, primarily because William had to abandon his campaign in France because Northern England came under attack from Malcolm III of Scotland. The invasion of the Scots was repulsed, and Carlisle Castle was built by the Normans to have stronger control over the areas claimed by Malcolm III (Cumberland and Westmorland). In 1093, the ambitious King of the Scots invaded again and ravaged Northumbria for some time, until he was killed together with his son and heir at the Battle of Alnwick (13 November 1093). The throne of Scotland was then seized by Malcolm's brother, Donald (c. 1032–1099), but William II did not recognise the latter's ascendancy. The main reasoning for this was the hope that

Knight wearing a mask helmet. (Sericum et ferrum)

the Scots could be weakened by provoking a civil war between two opposing pretenders, and so William first supported the claims of Malcolm's son Duncan (c.1060–12 November 1094) and then of another of Malcolm's sons, named Edgar (c.1074–8 January 1107). The latter, during 1094–1097, fought against his uncle Donald with the support of the Normans and was finally able to obtain the throne of his father. After becoming absolute ruler of Scotland, Edgar ceded Lothian to William II and attended the latter's court. William II was the first English monarch to play a significant role in the internal politics of Scotland and try to extend his influence north of Northumbria. He was also the first King of England to campaign in Wales. The latter Celtic country was still fully independent from England, and thus William II had to secure his control over the border, dividing his lands from the Welsh ones. He conducted two forays into Wales during 1097 and built a series of castles along the border, which became the backbone of the future 'Marcher Lordships', the border fiefdoms assigned to the most warlike Norman nobles.

In 1096, Robert Curthose, who had been suffering a loss of prestige from his younger brother's successes, decided to join the First Crusade, and, to fund his venture, he decided to lend the Duchy of Normandy to William II in return for the payment of 10,000 marks. The King of England took the opportunity represented by his brother's unexpected offer and levied a special tax in his realm in order to pay the sum requested by Robert. As a result, after Robert left Europe for the Holy Land, William II started to rule Normandy as regent. The King of England did his best to protect the borders of the duchy from the expansionist ambitions of the French monarchy: he campaigned on the continent twice (in 1097 and 1099) and obtained some positive results, securing Maine but failed to reconquer the portion of the Vexin region that had already been lost by the Normans during his father's late reign.

William II, like his predecessor on the English throne, was an excellent administrator and a skilled politician. In terms of the Church, both in England and on the continent, he was able to retain full control over his national clergy without coming into direct conflict with the papacy. During William's reign, Gregorian Reforms were trying to transform the Pope – at this time Pope Gregory VII (1073–1085) – into a real 'universal monarch' who exerted his power over all the Christian realms of Europe. William II managed to preserve the balance between the autonomy of his clergy and positive relations with the papacy. On 2 August 1100, while hunting near Brockenhurst, William II was shot by an arrow and killed by accident. The sudden death of the king took both his kingdom and his brothers by surprise. When

William II died, Robert Curthose was on his return journey from the First Crusade and was already raising funds to buy back his Duchy of Normandy. Robert, however, did not reach Normandy in time: his younger brother Henry, soon after William II's death, hastened to Winchester, where he secured possession of the royal treasury and then moved rapidly to London where he was crowned King of England on 5 August.

Upon his return to Normandy, Robert, urged by several Norman nobles who were sure that William II's death was the result of a plot orchestrated by Henry, claimed the English throne for himself and started to prepare an invasion of England. Henry, who had been crowned as Henry I, did his best to secure his control over England before the landing of his brother. He announced that he would abandon William II's rigid policies towards the Church that limited bishops' role in politics, promised to prevent royal abuses on the feudal lords' property rights and proclaimed that he would initiate a new age of peace for his realm. He gave lands and money to the major Norman aristocrats of England and – to secure his northern borders – married Matilda (1080–1 May 1118), daughter of Malcolm III of Scotland. By July 1101, Robert was ready to invade England with his army, while Henry was still experiencing serious military difficulties. Several of his major warlords had preferred not to join the royal army and instead wait and see how events developed. Only the contingents raised from the ecclesiastical landed properties went to the military camp built by the king, where they underwent basic training in view of the upcoming campaign. Robert Curthose

The magnificent enamel effigy from the tomb of Geoffrey Plantagenet in Le Mans. Geoffrey V (24 August 1113–7 September 1151), Count of Anjou and Duke of Normandy, is considered the real founder of the Plantagenet dynasty; by marrying Empress Matilda (7 February 1102–10 September 1167), he became a protagonist of the English political scene. His nickname of 'Plante Genest' or 'Planter of Broom' later started to identify the royal family initiated by his son Henry II. Since the Plantagenets' heartland was in Anjou, they were usually referred to as 'Angevins' in contemporary sources. The funerary plaque shown in this photo, commissioned by Empress Matilda, is one of the earliest examples of Medieval heraldry; on the kite shield of Geoffrey, it is possible to see six golden rampant lions placed in three horizontal rows (with three, two and one figure from top to bottom) over a medium blue background. This motif was granted to a young Geoffrey by Henry I of England in 1128, according to the chronicler Jean de Marmentier; it was later adopted by Geoffrey's grandson, William Longespée (c.1167–7 March 1226), and was probably the origin of the three golden lions of the Royal Arms of England. Geoffrey is depicted wearing a richly ornamented emerald green tunic and a light blue cloak; the Phrygian headgear, quite popular in northern France, has an embroidered golden lion. (Original creator of enamel unknown, Public domain, via Wikimedia Commons)

Knight of the 12th century. (Les Seigneurs d'Orient)

landed at Portsmouth on 20 July, at the head of an army that was small but well equipped; he was soon joined by several Norman aristocrats who supported his cause and enlarged his military forces. However, Robert, instead of marching on Winchester to seize the royal treasure, made the great mistake of waiting for the arrival of some more troops loyal to him. This enabled Henry to assemble his forces and move towards the invading army. The two opposing leaders met at Alton, in Hampshire; instead of fighting against each other, however, the two brothers initiated peace negotiations. Both were weak from a military point of view and thus were not sure about the outcome of an eventual pitched battle. The negotiations led to the signing of the Treaty of Alton, which stated that Robert recognised Henry as the legitimate King of England and Henry renounced all his claims on Normandy. Despite the treaty, the King of England inflicted severe penalties on the nobles who had stood against him during the invasion. In reality, Henry I had only signed the Treaty of Alton to gain some time and to secure his political position in England; he never abandoned the idea of conquering the Duchy of Normandy from his brother.

During the years 1103–1104, Henry allied himself with the most powerful aristocrats of Normandy, offering them lands and titles in exchange for their loyalty. He was progressively isolating his brother, who could now count on very few military resources. In 1105, after Robert Curthose had been abandoned by most of his previous supporters, Henry I sent a token force of knights to Normandy in order to provoke a confrontation with his brother. When these knights were captured by Robert, Henry launched his invasion of the duchy. The 1105 campaign in Normandy was a failure for the King of England, who captured some important cities but was not able to defeat his brother. In 1106, Henry I invaded again, this time at the head of a larger force. In September of that year, the decisive confrontation of the campaign took place at Tincherbray: Robert attacked first with his cavalry, but Henry responded with his reserve forces commanded by his French allies, the Count of Maine and the Duke of Brittany. Robert was defeated and taken prisoner. After crushing any form of resistance in Normandy, Henry sent his older brother to Devizes

Miniature from the folio 24 recto of the Morgan Bible, depicting a king and his most important vassals at court. The feudal military system of the Plantagenet Empire was based on the loyalty of the nobles towards their monarch and was greatly influenced by the political attitude of the barons. The Morgan Bible was produced in France during the 1240s. (Public domain, The Morgan Library and Museum)

Castle in Wiltshire, where he was imprisoned for two decades before being moved to Cardiff, where he died as a captive in 1134 (just a few months before his younger brother). After the events of 1106, the Duchy of Normandy and the Kingdom of England were ruled by the same monarch until the Norman Dynasty came to an end. The fact that Normandy and England were again under the control of a single ruler caused the same issues for Henry I as it had for his father William the Conqueror, because the new King of France – Louis VI (late 1081–1 August 1137), ruling since 1108 – also had concrete plans to assert his power over the most important French feudal lords (including the Duke of Normandy). Louis

Miniature from the folio 32 verso of the Morgan Bible, representing a milite (right) with his squire (left). The knight has full armour and is travelling with his 'courser', a strong horse of good quality being inferior to the 'destrier' employed in battle but superior to the all-purpose 'rouncey'. The squire, wearing a 'chapel de fer', is transporting the spear of his lord. (Public domain, The Morgan Library and Museum)

demanded Henry give homage to him as any other vassal of the French crown; the King of England refused, and the situation soon seemed to be on the verge of the outbreak of a new war. After both sides mobilised their military forces along the borders of Normandy, the crisis was resolved with peace negotiations; this led to the stipulation of a temporary truce, leaving the most important existing issues completely unresolved. In 1111, taking advantage of a new feudal rebellion that was taking place in France against Louis VI, Henry I landed in Normandy at the head of an army and joined his forces with those of the French nobles who were fighting against the central government. In March 1113, after having suffered several defeats, Louis decided to end the hostilities and negotiated a peace settlement with Henry. The latter was given some disputed fortresses located on Normandy's borders and was confirmed as the feudal overlord of Maine.

While these events took place on the continent, the situation on the Welsh border of England was deteriorating. In 1108, Henry I had conducted his first major campaign in Wales, which had a reasonably positive outcome and resulted in the Norman colonisation of the area around Pembroke. In 1114, however, the newly settled Norman lords were attacked by some of the most important Welsh leaders. To restore order in the Welsh Marches, Henry sent three armies into Wales and asked for the help of the King of Scotland Alexander I, (c. 1080—April 1124), one of his allies at the time. The campaign was a success for the Norman monarch, but the Welsh military forces had not been decisively defeated; the Welsh Marches came back under firm English control – with the addition of some new castles – but no other Welsh lands could be conquered by Henry I. Over time, especially after 1115, the King of England became increasingly concerned about his succession. He wanted to have his son, William Adelin (5 August 1103–25 November 1120), recognised as the future legitimate Duke of Normandy by Louis VI. The latter, however, refused all Henry I's offers and declared that the legitimate future Duke of Normandy was William Clito (25 October 1102–28 July 1128), son of Robert Curthose. Because of this, in 1116, hostilities resumed between Henry I and Louis VI. The numerical superiority of the enemy obliged the King of England to adopt a defensive strategy, which resulted in Louis' army pillaging a large portion of the Norman countryside. During 1118, most of the Norman nobles fighting in northern France abandoned Henry and changed side, but the king continued to resist his enemies. In 1119, at the Battle of Brémule in Vexin, Henry I and Louis VI fought against each other on the open field. The King of England, against all odds, was able to prevail and to obtain a great victory. After the success of Brémule, the hostilities in France slowly came to an end, with the final signing of a peace treaty. According to this, William Adelin was recognised as the future legitimate Duke of Normandy in exchange for accepting to give homage to Louis VI.

Henry I was an excellent monarch in many ways. Like his father, he spent most of his life travelling across his domains and created an itinerant royal court made up of various components: the chapel – headed by the chancellor – looked after the royal documents; the chamber dealt with financial affairs; and the office of the master-marshal, responsible for logistical and military matters. The court or 'familia regis' also included the elite knights of the royal household, who obeyed the king's direct orders and followed him to every corner of his domain. Henry I was responsible for the development of the Royal Exchequer, which collected and audited the revenues sent by the sheriffs from the various shires. 'Eyre' or itinerant courts of justice came into being and many new laws were promulgated during Henry's long reign. The monarch also reformed coinage three times and introduced new administrative institutions – similar to the English ones – in Normandy. Soon after it seemed that the peace agreements of 1120 had resolved his succession problems, however, a tragedy shocked Henry's life. His son and successor William Adelin died in the sinking of the royal vessel known as the 'White Ship' on 25 November 1120. This unexpected event left Henry I with no legitimate son; as a result, the monarch announced his intention to take a new wife, Adeliza of Louvain, in order to produce a new heir. The death of William Adelin, however, destroyed the delicate balance of power that Henry had created with such difficulty in northern France. His French enemies encouraged a new rebellion of the Norman aristocrats and attacked the borders of the Duchy of Normandy. During 1123–1124, the King of England had to send most of his forces to the continent and conduct some costly campaigns against his local enemies. In the end, however, the feudal revolt in Normandy was crushed. By 1125, the old king was yet to conceive any new children, and the future of his dynasty appeared to be at risk.

Knight of the 12th century wearing a 'great helmet'. (Les Seigneurs d'Orient)

Chapter 4
The Anarchy
1135–1154

Henry I had a legitimate daughter, Matilda, but in Medieval Europe it was very uncommon to see a woman inheriting a throne. However, as Henry failed to produce a male heir in the years that followed 1120, he designated Matilda as his successor, despite the opposition of a good portion of the English nobility. After having been married to Henry V (Aug 11, 1086–May 23, 1125), King of Germany and monarch of the Holy Roman Empire, Empress Matilda remarried in 1128 to one of the most powerful French nobles: Geoffrey V, Count of Anjou (24 August 1113–7 September 1151). Geoffrey controlled a very large territory in northwestern France and was one of the King of France's most powerful vassals. The County of Anjou bordered the Duchy of Normandy and the Angevins had been the worst enemies of the Normans for a long time. The border between Normandy and Anjou had been the theatre of several battles between the two aristocratic families and thus Geoffrey V was hated by a good portion of England's Norman nobility. The old Henry I tried his best to secure the loyalty of his aristocrats towards Matilda: he obliged the English nobles to swear their allegiance to her on three occasions, but these formalities did little to change the situation. Geoffrey V had very ambitious political plans: he wanted to unite England, Normandy and Anjou into a single 'Angevin Empire' stretching from the southern borders of Scotland to the very heart of France. He, however, was impatient and pressed the old Henry I with his requests. This led to the souring of relations between the English king and his daughter Matilda, since Henry understood that the Angevins wanted to occupy Normandy before his death, which did not look imminent. As a result, when a minor revolt broke out in southern Normandy, Matilda and her husband joined the rebels: Henry went to France as the head of a military force with the objective of crushing the rebellious couple, but died before encountering them on the field of battle during 1135. At this point, a real succession crisis began: Matilda had revolted against her father, but from a formal point of view she was still the legitimate heir of Henry. Most of the English nobles, however, had no intention of supporting her.

As a result of this situation, before Matilda and Geoffrey could take action, the English nobles crowned a new Norman king: Stephen of Blois (c.1097–Oct 25 1154). He was the son of Adela of Normandy (c.1067–8 March 1137), a daughter of William the Conqueror who had married Stephen Henry of Blois (c.1045–19 May 1102), one of the most powerful nobles of northern France. Stephen was not the eldest son of Stephen Henry and thus had no chance of inheriting his father's French territories; as a result, since childhood, he had lived at Henry I's court as a client of the king and took part in several of the military campaigns conducted by his uncle. In 1125, Stephen had married Matilda of Boulogne (c.1105–3 May 1152), the daughter and only heir of the Duke of Boulogne. The duke was a very important French aristocrat, who also owned large territorial domains in Southern England. By Henry I's death, Stephen of Blois had become a respected member of the English court and his younger brother, Henry (c.1096–8 August 1171), had risen to prominence after becoming the Bishop of Winchester. Thanks to the support of his wife and of his brother, as well as of the Norman aristocrats, Stephen was chosen as the new King of England. Initially, Matilda and Geoffrey were blocked in southern Normandy by the royal army that had been raised by Henry I, and could not

Battle of knights from a miniature of the Codex Manesse. This was produced in Germany during the early 14th century. (Master of the Codex Manesse, Public domain, via Wikimedia Commons)

move to England to claim the vacant throne. Stephen, in contrast, sailed from Boulogne to his future realm very rapidly. Thanks to his brother Henry, he could count on the support of the Church, and thanks to the unpopularity of Geoffrey he was acclaimed by the population of London. In exchange for the Archbishop of Canterbury's support for his succession to the throne, Stephen granted extensive freedoms and liberties to the Church, and in a few weeks, shortly after his coronation, the new English monarch was able to obtain the support of all the major nobles. Very soon, however, he had to march north in order to defend the borders of his new realm. After hearing of Henry I's death, David I of Scotland (c.1084–24 May 1153) had attacked Northern England with the objective of conquering some border fortifications and using the political turmoil taking place in London to his advantage. The Scottish troops obtained a series of minor successes during the early phase of this border conflict, since they occupied several strongholds located along the frontier, together with Carlisle and Newcastle. At that time, the exact border between the Scottish Lowlands and Northern England was not yet defined: David I, for example, considered both Cumberland and Northumbria as part of his personal domains and was determined to conquer them. Stephen of Blois marched north at the head of his royal army but preferred to avoid a pitched battle with the Scottish troops; he was well aware that Matilda and Geoffrey were probably going to invade England and thus could not initiate a bloody war with Scotland. Stephen and David eventually agreed to compromise: the Scottish monarch would obtain the possession of Carlisle but would renounce all the other frontier territories that he had conquered during the previous weeks. After obtaining this diplomatic success, Stephen held his first royal court at Easter and invited most of the Anglo-Norman nobles. Many aristocrats and officials of the Church gathered at Westminster, where the king issued a new royal charter that confirmed all the promises already made to the Church. The new monarch also promised to cancel all the royal abuses, such as arbitrary confiscation of goods, that had become increasingly common during the last years of Henry I's reign. Numerous grants of land and favours were given out by the king to the aristocrats who were present at the Easter court, and he also endowed numerous church foundations by giving further lands to the clergy. Stephen could also count on the support of Louis VI, who was a personal enemy of Geoffrey of Anjou and who wanted to avoid the formation of an Angevin Empire stretching across the English Channel. As a result, by the end of 1136, his succession to the English throne had been recognised as legitimate by Louis VI as well as by Pope Innocent II (died 24 September 1143), who was impressed by the many privileges conceded to the Church by the new monarch.

During 1136, Stephen experienced serious troubles in Wales, where his military positions were not particularly stable. As previously discussed, at the time of William the Conqueror's arrival in England, Wales was still divided into a series of princedoms that were dominated by local warlords. William never attempted to annex Wales to his new dominions but simply adopted a defensive strategy in order to stop the incursions of the Welsh warriors. This was based on the creation of a series of earldoms in the borderlands, possession of which was given to the most warlike Norman nobles. These earldoms became known as the 'Welsh Marches' and worked as a sort of 'buffer zone' between England and Wales. The Norman warlords of the Welsh Marches were given special powers by William and could count on significant military forces; they did not limit themselves to the static defence of their territories but gradually started to penetrate into the southeastern territories of Wales. During Henry I's reign, several Norman castles were built in the border areas of Wales, but due to the resistance of the local population the English penetration in the region was never stablised. Following Henry I's death, the Welsh warriors started to launch new attacks against the English territories and several minor revolts broke out in those portions of Wales that were under English control. During the early days of January

Battle of knights from a miniature of the Codex Manesse. Note the complexity of the heraldic motifs. (Master of the Codex Manesse, Public domain, via Wikimedia Commons)

Battle of knights from a miniature of the Codex Manesse. Note the presence of a military banner. (Master of the Codex Manesse, Public domain, via Wikimedia Commons)

1136, the Welsh military forces obtained a clear victory over the English at the Battle of Llwchwr, during which around 500 of Stephen's men were killed. The Welsh, like David I of Scotland, wanted to use the complicated political situation of England to their advantage and hoped to expel the foreign invaders from their border lands. Most of the Welsh princes/warlords temporarily put aside their internal rivalries and joined forces to pursue a common goal. A Welsh military force of 6,000 men was assembled, including 2,000 cavalrymen equipped with chainmail like their Norman opponents; this army was able to obtain a great victory over the local English forces at the Battle of Crug Mawr (October 1136) and even burned the town of Cardigan (which was one of the main English military bases in Wales). Due to these unexpected setbacks, by the end of 1137, Stephen of Blois abandoned any hope of putting down the rebellion in Wales, as he had to focus on the defence of his main possessions from the attacks of Geoffrey of Anjou. The latter had started his offensives against the Duchy of Normandy during the early months of 1136, raiding and burning on an extensive scale rather than attempting a permanent occupation of the Norman lands. In 1137, Stephen went to Normandy to meet with his older brother Theobald (1090–1152), who was now the Count of Blois, and with the King of France, Louis VI. Both supported Stephen and encouraged him to take the initiative against the Angevins. The English monarch, however, soon showed all his military deficiencies: he had to recruit a very large contingent of Flemish mercenaries in order to field a significant army in France and was not able to keep order among the ranks of his troops. The frictions between his Norman feudal contingents and the Flemish mercenaries soon transformed into violent combat that led to the desertion of most of the Normans. Due to this situation, Stephen had no choice but to agree a truce with Geoffrey, promising to pay him 2,000 marks a year in exchange for peace on the borders of Normandy. The military events that had taken place in Wales and France during 1137 had shown all the limits of the new English king.

In 1138, Robert of Gloucester (c.1090–31 October 1147), an illegitimate son of Henry I as well as one of the most powerful Anglo-Norman nobles, rose up in revolt against Stephen, initiating a long period of civil wars for England. He declared his support for Empress Matilda and Geoffrey and organised a regional rebellion in Kent from his personal dominions in France. Soon after these events, Geoffrey of Anjou renewed his attacks against southern Normandy and David I of Scotland invaded Northern England again with the objective of penetrating into Yorkshire. The Scottish monarch, who had previously recognised the succession of Stephen as legitimate, changed side and started to support Matilda and Geoffrey. Stephen had to face a very complex military situation and decided to concentrate all his efforts in England: he sent his wife to Kent with an expedition coming from Boulogne in order to reconquer the key port of Dover, and moved some of his best knights to Northern England in order to slow down the advance of David. In the northern territories, the English resistance was guided by Thurstan (c.1070–6 February 1140), the Archbishop of York. He was able to assemble an army of 10,000 men, who defeated the 16,000 Scottish invaders at the Battle of the Standard (22 August 1138). This blocked David's penetration into Yorkshire but left most of Cumberland and Northumbria under Scottish control. Meanwhile, Stephen went to Wales in order to re-establish his defences in the Welsh Marches. He obtained some minor successes, but did not defeat the Welsh princes in a definitive way. During the last months of 1138, Matilda of Boulogne was able to reconquer Dover and find a temporary agreement with the Scottish king (formalised in the so-called 'Treaty of Durham'): David remained in control of Carlisle and Cumberland, while his son and heir Henry was given Northumberland as a vassal of Stephen. Stephen retained possession of the vital castles of Bamburgh and Newcastle, but had renounced a large portion of Northern England in order to 'stabilise' his political position. The Treaty of Durham led to two decades of peace on the Anglo-Scottish border, but caused great malcontent among the powerful Norman nobles of Northern England, who hoped that Stephen could defeat David and

Heavy infantryman (left) and knight (right). (Historia Aquitanorum)

reconquer all the lost territories. One of these was Ranulf (1099–1153), Earl of Chester, who considered Carlisle and Cumberland as part of his personal dominions. Displeased by the conduct of his king, this powerful noble gradually reduced his support for Stephen's cause.

By the beginning of 1139, a full invasion of the Kingdom of England by Matilda and Geoffrey seemed imminent; by this time, the pair had been able to occupy most of Normandy and had been mobilising substantial military forces jointly with Robert of Gloucester. Stephen knew that the only way to retain control over his realm was to form a strong political alliance with the most important aristocrats, who would provide most of the king's troops in the case of invasion. Stephen created a large number of new earldoms, possession of which was given to the aristocrats who were willing to support the ruling monarch in the civil war. Most of the new earls were experienced military commanders, who were deployed in the most vulnerable parts of England and given additional powers by the king that allowed them to autonomously levy troops. Their main task, after the landing of Matilda's troops, was putting up a first line of defence against the invaders, as well as raising substantial military contingents for Stephen. The latter also removed several bishops who were favourable to Matilda and Geoffrey, and held large territorial possessions; this caused several incidents when some of the bishops tried to resist and damaged Stephen's relationship with part of the English clergy. In August of 1139, Matilda and Geoffrey's invasion finally materialised. Baldwin de Revers (died 4 June 1155), one of Matilda's best military commanders, crossed the English Channel and landed in Wareham with the objective of capturing a major port so that the bulk of Geoffrey's troops could disembark. Stephen's military forces, however, were able to contain Baldwin de Revers and no major port was occupied. On 30 September, Matilda and Robert of Gloucester landed at Arundel in West Sussex with a small contingent of just 140 knights. The local castle became their main base, where Matilda installed a sort of 'provisional court'. Robert soon moved northwest to reach Wallingford and Bristol, having the task of raising popular support for Matilda as well as linking up with the rebels who operated in Gloucester. Stephen's response to his enemies was rapid: he marched south and besieged the castle of Arundel, trapping Matilda inside. At this point, thanks to the mediation of Henry of Blois, a temporary truce was signed between the

Heavy infantryman. (Milites Pagenses)

two warring parties. Matilda was released from the siege of Arundel and was allowed to unite her forces with those of Robert of Gloucester. The reasons behind Stephen's decision to release Matilda were twofold: firstly, he knew it was unlikely he could secure the castle of Arundel quickly, and a long siege would only have damaged his cause; secondly, the main military threat to the stability of his rule was represented by Robert of Gloucester and not by Matilda, who had just a few knights under her command in Arundel.

The months that followed these events were positive for Matilda, since her ally Robert was able to expand his military control over a vast area of England that stretched from Gloucester to Cornwall and from the Welsh Marches to Oxford. Matilda's new provisional court was established in Gloucester, not

Knight accompanied by two heavy infantrymen. (Historia Aquitanorum)

far from the main stronghold of Robert in Bristol. In this phase of the civil war, Stephen tried to protect the city of London from an eventual attack and thus besieged the important castle of Wallingford in order to obtain control over the so-called 'Thames Corridor'. The fortification, however, was well defended and the king was unable to take it. Part of the royal army was left at Wallingford in order to blockade the garrison of the castle, while Stephen and the majority of his troops attacked some other minor castles in the Wiltshire area. The king's incursions, however, did not last for long because an enemy attack against his troops in Wallingford forced him to come back to defend London. The following months of stalemate were very costly for the king: he did not have the needed economic resources to conduct a long conflict, and several of the most important nobles were already ready to abandon him at the first opportune moment. In the early weeks of 1140, Nigel (c.1100–1169), Bishop of Ely, rebelled against Stephen in retaliation for the confiscations that he had suffered during the previous year. The king responded rapidly to this new threat, before Nigel could join forces with Robert of Gloucester. The bishop's main base was on the Isle of Ely, which was surrounded by protective fenland; Stephen took his military forces into the fens and built a temporary bridge made of boats lashed together that enabled him to launch a surprise assault on the island. Nigel was utterly defeated but was able to save his life.

While these events took place in the eastern regions of England, the military situation started to change also along the northern borders of the kingdom. Ranulf of Chester decided to act against Prince Henry of Scotland in order to gain control over a vast portion of Northern England. Prince Henry was one of Stephen's strongest supporters by now, as he knew that, in case of Matilda's victory, he would lose all the English lands that were under his control. Ranulf first tried to kill Prince Henry by organising an ambush against him and then launched a surprise attack against the castle of Lincoln, which was held by Stephen's men. The king marched north with his troops but instead of fighting against the rebel noble he agreed to a truce with him. Ranulf was allowed to retain control over the castle of Lincoln in exchange for siding with Stephen in the ongoing civil war. The truce, however, did not last long: as soon as the royal army left Northern England, Ranulf proclaimed his support for Matilda. At this point, Stephen gathered his military forces again and marched north once more in order to place the castle of Lincoln under siege. In the early weeks of 1141, while the king was with his troops around Lincoln, Robert of Gloucester joined forces with Ranulf of Chester and marched against Stephen with the objective of fighting a large pitched battle. The king held a council to decide whether to face the enemy or to wait for the arrival of some reinforcements. In the end, Stephen decided to fight, and the Battle of Lincoln (2 February 1141) took place. Like most of the battles in England at this time, it was an affair between two small groups of heavily equipped knights: Stephen had 1,250 combatants (mostly experienced knights), while Robert of Gloucester and Ranulf of Chester had gathered around 1,000 men (a portion of whom were Welsh warriors). As soon as the clash began, most of the royalist nobles abandoned their king with their knights and changed side; Robert of Gloucester launched a frontal cavalry charge and Stephen was captured. The Battle of Lincoln was a disaster for the king, who was imprisoned in Bristol.

Matilda was now free to take all the necessary steps to have herself crowned, and thus she made a deal with Henry of Blois. The latter agreed to abandon his brother Stephen in exchange for receiving complete control over the clergy of England once Matilda was crowned. A good portion of the aristocracy and the most important exponents of the Church were now favourable to Matilda, but the same could not be said for the population of London. The future queen, in fact, was generally perceived as a 'stranger' because of her husband. When Matilda advanced to London to stage her coronation in June, the city rose up in revolt, and she was forced to flee after being taken by surprise and made a chaotic retreat to Oxford. While these events took place in England, Geoffrey of Anjou had continued fighting in France to complete his conquest of Normandy. The duchy was almost defenceless, because the political situation of France had changed dramatically from the previous years. Theobald, Stephen's powerful brother, could no longer intervene to defend Normandy, since he had to defend his own territories from the expansionism of the new French monarch, Louis VII (1120–18 September 1180). Geoffrey's successes in the duchy, however, were perceived as a dangerous threat by many Anglo-Norman nobles who owned lands in England as well as in Normandy. With Matilda's victory, they stood to lose their French territories forever, since the new queen would grant the Normandy lands to her husband. Furthermore, as long as the king was taken captive rather than killed, his cause remained alive. Matilda of Boulogne, Stephen's wife, played a crucial role in this phase of the civil war. She gathered all the military forces that were still loyal to the king and marched to London, where the population was favourable to the royalist cause. After the rebellion of London, Henry of Blois decided to terminate his collaboration with Matilda

Heavy infantryman equipped with nasal helmet. (Historia Aquitanorum)

and changed side again. He met with Matilda of Boulogne and transferred his support to her. Following their retreat from London, Robert of Gloucester and Matilda decided to attack Henry of Blois after Henry expressed his loyalty towards Stephen. Henry's episcopal castle of Winchester was besieged, but very soon the attackers were surrounded by the military forces assembled by Matilda of Boulogne. The besiegers then divided into two parts: one, commanded by Matilda, left the siege and fled; the other, commanded by Robert, remained to fight but was completely defeated by the royalist military forces. In this so-called 'Rout of Winchester', Robert of Gloucester was captured.

During November of 1141, the two warring sides exchanged their two military leaders: Stephen returned to London while Robert joined Matilda in Oxford. With his brother's support, Stephen was crowned again, alongside with his wife Matilda of Boulogne, in December. During the early months of 1142, after a period of illness, Stephen travelled to Northern England and had a meeting with the turbulent Ranulf of Chester. After some complex negotiations, he was finally convinced to join the king and changed his loyalties once again. The summer of 1142 saw Stephen besieging some newly built enemy castles like those of Cirencester, Bampton and Wareham; meanwhile Robert of Gloucester had left England and had gone to France with part of his military forces in order to assist Geoffrey in his operations in Normandy. Robert was sure that Matilda would have been able to retain Oxford while he was away, since the city was protected by strong walls and the Isis River. Contrary to all expectations, however, Stephen launched a surprise attack against Oxford by swimming with some of his troops across the Isis. The attack was a great

Heavy infantryman from the 11th century. (Historia Aquitanorum)

success, and the city was taken rapidly; Matilda was trapped inside her Oxford castle and risked full capture. Her fortress, however, was very strong and Stephen was in no position to mount an assault against it. The king, rather than storming the castle, settled down for a long siege with the firm intention of capturing Matilda. Against all odds, the latter was able to escape from the besieged fortification just before Christmas without being intercepted by the royal troops. The day following this unexpected event, the garrison of the castle surrendered, but Stephen had not achieved his main objective of capturing Matilda. After obtaining a series of victories in France, Robert of Gloucester returned to England at the head of some substantial military forces and took the initiative. He attacked the castle of Wilton, which was an important base of the royalist troops in Herefordshire. Stephen was besieged in Wilton and thus had no choice but to fight a new pitched battle against his enemies. He tried to emerge from the fortress, but was stopped by a frontal cavalry charge led by Robert. The king was on the verge of being captured for a second time, but in the end he was able to flee from the battlefield. The Battle of Wilton had been a defeat for the royalists, but not a decisive one. However, during the late months of 1143, Stephen had to face a new military threat, which was represented by the rebellion of the Earl of Essex, Geoffrey de Mandeville II (died September 1144). The latter had been obliged by the king to give up many of his fortifications in London during the previous years, including the Tower of London. When the right moment came, the Earl of Essex rebelled against the king and launched a military campaign from the Isle of Ely (where he had his main base). Stephen did not have the resources to crush this new enemy, but was able to limit the incursions launched against London. In September 1144, the Earl of Essex died during a raid on Burwell and thus his rebellion came to a sudden end. During 1145, the main conflict continued with some victories for the king, who recaptured the castle of Farringdon in Oxfordshire and also captured Ranulf of Chester. The latter had to hand over several of his most important castles in order to avoid execution, and, as a result, Stephen regained control over the important fortifications of Lincoln and Coventry. Ranulf rebelled again as soon as he was relieved from captivity, and the political situation of Northern England remained particularly unstable.

If the situation of Matilda's cause in England was still far from decisive, the same could not be said for France: there, her husband Geoffrey had taken the very important city of Rouen and had been recognised as the Duke of Normandy. In 1147, Robert of Gloucester died from natural causes and Matilda decided to abandon England; as a result, the military operations lost most of their intensity and many aristocrats of the opposing factions started to make individual peace agreements between themselves. After Matilda's return to Normandy, her young son Henry landed in England at the head of a small mercenary contingent, but this expedition failed quite rapidly. In 1149, Henry returned to England, this time with the intention of forming an alliance with Ranulf of Chester; the plan worked, and an attack against the city of York was organised. Stephen, however, quickly marched north to face this new menace and prevented his enemies from taking York. Defeated without fighting for the second time, the young Henry returned to Normandy.

The son of Matilda and Geoffrey was made Duke of Normandy soon after, and subsequently started to be seen by many as the best possible heir to the throne of England. In 1152, he married Eleanor (c.1122–1 April 1204), Duchess of Aquitaine, who had recently had her marriage to Louis VII of France annulled and who controlled some very large territorial domains. This union made Henry the future ruler of a huge portion of France and one of the most powerful aristocrats in Europe. Stephen, after many years of battles, was growing old and was starting to plan the succession to his throne. His eldest son Eustace (c.1129/1131–17 August 1153) had already been given the County of Boulogne in 1147, and Stephen wanted to crown him in Westminster while he himself was still alive. In 1152, at Easter, the king gathered the English nobles in order to have them swear fealty to Eustace and asked the bishops of his realm to crown his eldest son as his successor to the throne of England. The clergy, however, won over by Matilda and Geoffrey's promises of new clerical land and properties, were against Eustace's rise to power and the bishops opposed Stephen's plans in every possible way. In 1153, Henry returned to England for the

Heavy infantryman wearing a decorated version of a nasal helmet. (Milites Pagenses)

third time at the head of a small army; he besieged the castle of Malmesbury but avoided fighting a pitched battle against the king when he tried to intercept him along the Avon River. Henry did not achieve any significant military success, but an increasing number of nobles began to join his cause. Stephen tried to restore order among his aristocrats by besieging the important castle of Wallingford, which had fallen into rebel hands. However, the siege failed thanks to Henry and his small army. The two opponents confronted each other across the River Thames at Wallingford, but no real battle took place, since the nobles of both sides had no intention of fighting. A truce was brokered, and a private meeting took place between Stephen and Henry; to many contemporary observers, it seemed that the old king was now ready to cede his throne to Matilda's son. A few months later, Eustace died, removing the most important claimant to the English throne and allowing for an important step towards a real pacification of the realm. The hostilities continued for some time, however, and saw Henry conquering Oxford as well as Stamford, but Henry of Blois and Archbishop Theobald of Canterbury were now working to broker a permanent peace settlement between the two opposing sides. After a new meeting between Stephen and Henry, the Treaty of Winchester was signed and the long civil war finally came to an end in 1153: Stephen adopted Henry as his son and successor, in return for Henry paying formal homage to him. The king's remaining son, William, renounced his claims to the English throne and recognised Henry as the future monarch. Stephen and Henry sealed the treaty with a famous 'kiss of peace' in Winchester Cathedral, and, on 25 October 1154, just a few months after putting an end to the civil war, Stephen of Blois died.

Heavy infantryman from the 11th century. (Historia Aquitanorum)

Henry was crowned King of England and the new Plantagenet Dynasty obtained control over the realm.

To us, King Henry II, son of Matilda and Geoffrey, was the first Plantagenet king of England, but at the time of his accession to the throne, the royal family to which he belonged was still simply known as the Angevins. Furthermore, the monarchs who followed Henry II (starting from his sons Richard the Lionheart and John Lackland) are usually referred to as Angevin kings in the English contemporary sources. It was only with Richard of York (21 September 1411–30 December 1460), in the 15th century, that the English royal family adopted the new denomination of 'Plantagenets', and the name was applied retroactively to all the English monarchs who came after Stephen of Blois. The first three exponents of the new dynasty are still commonly known as 'Angevin' kings because of their important political interests/territorial possessions in France and their strong links to their home region of Anjou. The term 'Plantagenet' derived from the French nickname 'Plante Genest' that was attributed to Geoffrey of Anjou. 'Genest' was the French version of the Latin word 'Genista', which was used to indicate the flowering plant that we know as Scotch Broom. The nickname 'Plante Genest', meant 'the man who plants a Scotch Broom'. We don't know if Geoffrey of Anjou really had a passion for this plant, but in any case, Richard of York decided to create a new name for his family from the nickname of his ancestor. It is fair to say that the first three 'Plantagenet' monarchs of England had a distinct 'Angevin' character, while their successors were more 'English' in nature.

Heavy infantryman bearing sword and kite shield. (Historia Aquitanorum)

Above left: Heavy infantryman armed with axe. (Les Guerriers du Moyen-Age)

Above right: Heavy infantryman wearing a taller version of the chapel de fer helmet. (Les Guerriers du Moyen-Age)

Chapter 5
The Reign of Henry II
1154–1189

After Stephen of Blois' sudden death, Henry II took oaths of loyalty from some of the most important English aristocrats, who are usually referred to as 'barons' in medieval sources, and this is the term that is used in this book to indicate these warlike nobles of the realm. On 19 December 1154, Henry II was crowned at Westminster Abbey together with his wife Eleanor of Aquitaine. The first royal court was gathered in April of the following year, and this was the occasion for the new king to receive the formal submission of a large number of nobles. Henry II's political position had been reasonable since the beginning, because he had no potential rivals from a dynastic point of view except for Stephen's son William (c.1137–11 October 1159), who died early during Henry's reign. The new monarch, however, had inherited a devastated kingdom that had suffered a lot during the last decades of civil war: unauthorised castles had been built by many aristocrats in various parts of the countryside, brigandage was widespread in some regions and the rights of the Crown over common lands/forests were no longer respected by most of the population. The civil war, known as 'The Anarchy', had caused serious damages to the institutional structure created by William the Conqueror: even royal control over the coin mints had become limited, and this had important consequences for the financial capabilities of the Crown. Henry II ordered the demolition of many unauthorised castles, tried to restore the system of royal justice and attempted to reorganise the royal finances by collecting taxes in a more effective way. All these measures, however, were carried on from a distance by the king, as he spent six of his first eight years of reign in France and not in England. The new monarch had to face serious political troubles on the continent, but also on the borders of England, as both the King of Scotland and the Welsh warlords had taken advantage of the English political struggles to enlarge their territorial possessions. Henry II, who is often deemed a 'warrior king', soon tried to change the general situation existing on the field by limiting the ambitions of his rivals in the British Isles. In 1157, after having threatened to attack Scotland, Henry II obtained from the new monarch (the young Malcolm IV [1141–9 December 1165], grandson of David I) the return of all the lands of Northern England that had been occupied by Scottish troops during the English civil conflict. In Wales, Henry II conducted two military campaigns: one in the north (1157) and one in the south (1158); these resulted in the restoration of the status quo in the Welsh Marches but did not see the occupation of any new territory by the English.

Henry II experienced the most serious of his military problems in France, where he had a very difficult relationship with Louis VII. The latter feared that the 'Angevin Empire' could be a serious obstacle for the creation of a centralised monarchy in France and saw Henry II as a great rival. In his early life, Henry II had already clashed with Louis VII, because the latter did not want to recognise him as the legitimate Duke of Normandy; this situation worsened when Henry married Eleanor of Aquitaine, who had been Louis VII's previous wife and who controlled a large portion of French territory. Henry II created a strong network of alliances with some of the most important French nobles, in order to secure his dominion over Normandy and Anjou, and he created a military alliance with the Count of Flanders and with the Count of Blois. From a military point of view, Henry was much stronger than Louis, and as a result, the

Miniature from the folio 28 verso of the Morgan Bible, depicting the duel between David and Goliath. The former is represented as a peasant slinger of the feudal levy, armed only with a sling; the latter is equipped as a sergeant, with chapel de fer and padded poleyns (knee guards). (Public domain, The Morgan Library and Museum)

latter never tried to fight a full-scale war against the former. For many years, however, France lived in a state of constant tension, as the borders of the Angevin Empire were frequently raided by the nobles who were allied with Louis VII against Henry II. In 1154, soon after being crowned in Westminster, the new English king returned to France and concluded a peace treaty with Louis. He returned some territories to the French monarch but did not pay homage as a vassal of the French crown. In 1158, after some years of growing tension between the two kings, Henry II's eldest son, Henry (28 February 1155–11 June 1183), married Louis VII's daughter, Margaret. This union, however, did not end the ongoing 'cold war' between Henry and Louis.

The English monarch had a clear political plan in mind: he wanted to expand his territorial possessions in France as much as possible without fighting long wars. One of his primary targets was the Duchy of Brittany, located close to both England and Normandy. This was largely independent from the crown of France and had a very peculiar culture: Brittany, in fact, had been inhabited for a long time by Celtic communities that had a lot in common with the Welsh ones. It had been

Heavy infantryman wearing a chapel de fer helmet. (Les Guerriers du Moyen-Age)

annexed to France only by Charlemagne (after some very costly military campaigns conducted by the Franks). The Bretons had their own language and traditions, which were very different from those of mainland France. Like Wales, Brittany was divided into a series of small princedoms with warlike rulers who were never fully submitted to the central authority of the Duke. In 1148, Conan III (c.1096–17 September 1148), Duke of Brittany, died and a civil war broke out in the region. Henry II claimed to be the overlord of Brittany, since the latter had owed loyalty to his predecessor, Henry I, some decades before. As a result, he supported Conan IV's (c.1138–20 February 1171) claim as the new Duke of Brittany in the hope that he would be 'favourable' to him. With the progression of time, however, the pretender supported by Henry II changed his political line and started to struggle to preserve the autonomy of his homeland. As a result, the King of England changed his political approach and occupied the County of Nantes (located in the east of Brittany) in 1158. Louis VII of France did not intervene in the civil conflict of Brittany, at least directly, since the region was part of the Angevins' sphere of political influence.

Henry II did not only operate in Northern France but also in the south, where his objective was enlarging his wife's possessions in Aquitaine. During the previous years, the important city of Toulouse, which had always been part of the Duchy of Aquitaine, had started to be ruled as an independent county; Henry did not accept this, and thus undertook an important alliance with the main enemy of Toulouse: Raymond Berenguer of Barcelona (c.1114–6 August 1162). The Count of Toulouse, Raymond V (c.1134–c.1194), tried to preserve the independence of his territories by forming an alliance with Louis VII of France; he married the king's sister, Constance, in the hope of stopping Henry II's expansionism. The English king, however, attacked Toulouse and ravaged the countryside of the city before seizing some local castles and annexing the area of Quercy to Aquitaine. Once again, Louis VII refrained from intervening, but the tension between the two monarchs grew ever stronger.

After Henry II started to show his belligerency in Aquitaine also, Louis VII decided to reinforce his political position by forming some new alliances with important French aristocrats. After the death of his wife, he married the sister of the Count of Blois, Theobald V (1130–20 January 1191), and Champagne, Henry I (December 1127–16 March 1181), who were both extremely powerful and controlled two of France's richest regions. Theobald had previously been an ally of Henry II but was now getting increasingly worried about the expansionist ambitions of the Angevins. When Theobald mobilised his military forces along the border of Henry's French possessions, the English king responded by attacking the territory of Blois and conquering his rival's main castle, further souring relations. At the beginning of 1161, a total war between Henry II and Louis VII seemed inevitable, but during the following year a peace treaty was stipulated between the two kings through the mediation of Pope Alexander III. This simply cemented the situation existing on the field and could be considered as a personal victory by Henry II, as he had been able to expand and stabilise the Angevin Empire without fighting a large-scale war. However, Henry II's dominions did not have a coherent organisation and were not under the control of a single government: they consisted of a loose and highly flexible network of feudal connections that were all linked to the Angevin family. Henry travelled a lot across his 'empire', confirming his direct or indirect control over its various components and reforming the local governments in order to make them more efficient. Henry could count on the support of an emerging class of 'new men', minor aristocrats who were capable administrators and who rose to positions of prominence thanks to their personal loyalty towards the monarch. It was thanks to them that the Angevin Empire was kept together, despite the opposition of some barons.

In 1164, Louis VII of France started to enlarge his anti-Angevin coalition by forming an alliance with the Duchy of Burgundy as well as with the new Count of Flanders; the latter, unlike his predecessor, was concerned about Henry II's expansionist policies and thus preferred to side with the King of France. In 1165, the French monarch finally had a male heir, the future Philip Augustus (21 August 1165–14 July 1223), securing his dynasty against any future claim to his throne coming from the Angevins. Meanwhile, Henry II had started to exert a more direct control over Brittany, by launching a large-scale invasion of the region in 1166. The English king forced Conan IV to abdicate as duke and gave Brittany to Conan's daughter, Constance (c.1161–c.5 September 1201), who was betrothed to Henry II's son Geoffrey (23 September 1158–19 August 1186). With this move, the English king showed his firm intention to include Brittany among the territories of the Angevin Empire. Henry II also continued to act in other areas of France, most importantly in Aquitaine, where his struggle with Raymond of

Miniature from the folio 27 recto of the Morgan Bible, showing a mounted sergeant. Sometimes, the 'sergeants' – professional soldiers of great experience – were equipped exactly like the noble milites and had a personal squire like in this case. Note the use of a massive chapel de fer as well as metal plates acting as greaves. (Public domain, The Morgan Library and Museum)

Sergeant from the late 12th century; he is wearing iron greaves. (Les Guerriers du Moyen-Age)

Toulouse continued. Henry could now count on the support of the Archbishop of Bordeaux as well as of Alfonso II of Aragon (March 1157–25 April 1196); as a result, Raymond of Toulouse was forced to divorce Louis VII's sister and come under the political influence of Henry II.

In 1167, open war finally broke out between the Angevin monarch and the King of France. Louis VII allied himself with the Kingdom of Scotland, the Welsh princedoms and with the disgruntled Bretons in the hope of crushing the empire of his rival. Normandy was attacked by the French troops, but Henry II responded with a violent counter-attack that destroyed the main logistical base of his enemy at Chaumont-sur-Epte. After this defeat, before the war could become larger, Louis VII abandoned his allies and made a truce with the English king. After this, Henry was free to crush the Bretons and to restore his rule over their important duchy. In the following years, the English monarch became increasingly concerned about the succession to his throne and decided that his empire would be divided into three parts upon his death: his first son Henry would receive England and Normandy; Richard would be given the Duchy of Aquitaine; and Geoffrey would receive the Duchy of Brittany. In 1169, the king had a meeting with his old rival Louis VII at Montmirail; the French monarch recognised Henry II's plans for the division of his domains as legitimate, in exchange for being given formal homage from Henry II's sons. The years following the peace agreements of Montmirail saw the King of England reinforce his position in southern France, drawing up alliances with the Count of Savoy in the east, and with the King of Castile in the west. The daughter of the former was promised to Henry II's son John, while the latter married Henry II's daughter Eleanor (c. 1161–31 October 1214). Thanks to these intelligent diplomatic moves, in 1173, the King of England finally obtained the submission of Raymond of Toulouse and the city came under the influence of Aquitaine once more.

Henry II spent most of his life as a king dealing with French political concerns and only spent a limited portion of his time in England. However, he remains very well known in the British Isles mostly because of the controversial events that led to the assassination of Thomas Becket (21 December 1119/ 1120–29 December 1170). When the Archbishop of Canterbury, Theobald of Bec, died in 1161, Henry II saw an opportunity to reassert his royal rights over the Church in England. As previously discussed, the reign of Stephen of Blois had been a very positive period for a large portion of the English clergy, as they had been given many privileges in exchange for supporting Stephen's rise and permanence on the throne. Henry II chose Thomas Becket, his old friend and chancellor, as the new Archbishop of Canterbury, as the monarch

Above left: Sergeant from the late 12th century; he is armed with a falchion (one-handed, single-edged sword). (Les Guerriers du Moyen-Age)

Above right: Spearman with padded aketon. (De Gueules et d'Argent)

believed that Becket would remain extremely loyal to him. Henry's plans, however, did not work as expected: Becket changed his political ideas soon after becoming Archbishop and started to act as a fierce protector of the Church's rights in England. Becket tried to regain control over several lands that had been expropriated to the bishops by the royal government, and rallied against Henry's new taxation policies. Another source of conflict between the archbishop and the king was the treatment given to members of the clergy who committed secular crimes: according to Henry II's view, these individuals had to be judged by the royal courts like all the other subjects of the kingdom, but according to Becket's view, they could be judged only by clerical courts.

Spearman with nasal helmet. (De Gueules et d'Argent)

In 1164, under strong pressure from the king, the Archbishop of Canterbury was forced to accept the Constitutions of Clarendon, which gave to Henry II a legal basis to judge clergy in the royal courts. A few months after this, Thomas Becket fled to France, where he could count on the personal protection of Henry II's worst enemy: Louis VII. At this point, the King of England started to persecute Becket's supporters and the archbishop excommunicated all the religious or civil authorities who sided with the monarch. During this period, the papacy was dealing with a large number of troubles in Italy, since the Holy Roman Emperor Frederick I (December 1122–10 June 1190) was fighting against the Italian cities and the Papal States in order to exert more direct political control over the Italian peninsula. The ruling Pope, Alexander III, supported Becket in principle but was in no position to excommunicate the King of England, as the king could be an important ally for him in the ongoing struggle with Frederick I. In 1169, Henry II decided to crown his first son Henry as King of England and thus needed to make peace – at least temporarily – with the Archbishop of Canterbury. Becket, however, refused to reconcile himself with the king and Henry II's son had to be crowned by the Archbishop of York. At this point, the Pope authorised Becket to place an interdict on England to put some pressure on the king. In order to find a solution to the new crisis, Henry II agreed to come to terms with Becket, and the latter came back to England in December 1170. Once in the realm, however, the Archbishop of Canterbury excommunicated another three supporters of Henry II, infuriating the monarch. In response to this act, the king sent four of his knights to Canterbury with the order to arrest Becket for having broken his agreement with the Crown. The archbishop resisted arrest inside his cathedral and was killed by the royal knights. This event, unprecedented in the history of Christian Europe, horrified the Pope and the clergy of England. Becket was declared a martyr soon after his death and became a symbol of the Church's resistance against the attacks of the monarchies. Louis VII used this to his advantage in order to present Henry II as a violent man without moral principles. In a few months, the international pressure on the King of England grew immensely, and he was forced to negotiate a settlement with the Pope in May 1172. According to this, Henry II would organise a crusade to free the Holy Land from Islamic control, as well as overturning the Constitutions of Clarendon. The English monarch never went to the Holy Land, but he was able to restore his position in the eyes of the papacy without suffering further damages.

During the second half of his reign, Henry II spent most of his energy establishing some form of direct English control over Ireland. The three Norman kings and Stephen of Blois had never attempted to land on the island at the head of an army; they had plans to do so, especially William the Conqueror and Henry I, but their involvement on other fronts prevented them from taking action. By the time of Henry II's accession to the English throne, the territory of Ireland was controlled by a series of small kingdoms that were ruled by warlike princes. They were constantly at war against each other and could count – more or less – on similar military resources. The Kingdom of Leinster was the strongest of all, since it controlled a large portion of southern Ireland; its rulers were on good terms with Henry II even before 1154 but always remained fully independent from England. The Irish Church was completely autonomous from the English one, since it had not yet implemented the Gregorian Reforms that had been widely accepted in the rest of Europe. The Gaelic society of Ireland retained many pre-Christian features and feudalism had not yet been imported; as a result, the Irish princes and their subjects were very different from their English equivalents. From a formal point of view, the Archbishop of Canterbury had some claims to primacy over the Irish Church, and this was a strong factor behind Henry II's decision to invade Ireland. The English clergy wanted to impose the Gregorian Reform over the population of the island, which was depicted as barbarian and 'semi-pagan' by most of the contemporary English observers. The Anglo-Norman barons were also interested in the conquest of Ireland, since the occupation of new lands would give them new feudal possessions/titles.

In 1166, a coalition of Irish princedoms, led by the Kingdom of Connacht, attacked Leinster with the objective of ousting the local ruler Diarmait mac Murchada (c.1110–c.1 May 1171). The latter, after having been defeated, left Ireland and sought help from his ally Henry II. This provided Henry a legitimate opportunity to intervene in Ireland and gave Diarmait permission to recruit an army on his lands. Several English barons, mostly from the Welsh Marches, agreed to help the deposed King of Leinster by landing in Ireland with their military forces. Among them was Richard FitzGilbert de Clare (died 15 April 1136), famous by his nickname of 'Strongbow', to whom Diarmait had promised his

Spearman with large triangular shield. (De Gueules et d'Argent)

daughter's hand in marriage and the future kingship of Leinster. In May 1169, the English allies of Diarmait landed at Bannow Bay at the head of a force that comprised 40 knights, 60 men-at-arms and 360 archers. They were soon joined by 500 Irish warriors recruited by the deposed King of Leinster. The combined Anglo-Irish force besieged the seaport of Wexford and reconquered the whole Kingdom of Leinster before defeating the military forces of the neighbouring Kingdom of Ossory. After these events, the large coalition guided by the rulers of Connacht that had deposed Diarmait was re-formed and sent its troops back to Leinster. At this point, however, a peace agreement was ratified between the two warring sides: Diarmait was acknowledged as the legitimate King of Leinster in exchange for agreeing to send his English allies away from Ireland. Shortly after making peace with his enemies, however, Diarmait was reinforced by a new English expeditionary force and decided to march north from Leinster with the objective of raiding the countryside of Dublin. What had started as a simple English intervention in an Irish war was now becoming a full-scale invasion. In 1170, Strongbow landed at Passage with 1,200 men, 200 of whom were heavily armoured knights: they assaulted Waterford and conquered it after killing 700 Irish warriors. Diarmait then joined Strongbow at Waterford and the marriage between his daughter and the English warlord took place. Meanwhile, the Irish anti-Leinster coalition had been re-formed for the third time and was now ready to intercept the joint Anglo-Irish forces of Strongbow and Diarmait. The latter, however, bypassed the enemies by travelling over the Wicklow Mountains and reaching Dublin. The city was stormed and taken by surprise; this event was a

Miniature from the folio 27 verso of the Morgan Bible, showing the baggage train of a feudal army in the 13th century. The carts were used to transport all the equipment of troops, including helmets and chainmail; mules and donkeys were employed on a large scale, being fundamental elements of the military logistics system. The infantrymen coming from the feudal levies manned the carts and were tasked with transporting the various materials. Each 'battle' (division) of an army had its own distinctive banner, which was transported also on its carts in order to make them easily recognisable. The foot sergeant in the centre of the scene is very well equipped, with chapel de fer and padded aketon (including a specific protection for the neck); the standard-bearer on the right is wearing a 'corectum' (leather cuirass for the torso). (Public domain, The Morgan Library and Museum)

real turning point in the ongoing conflict, as it marked the beginning of a 'total war' in Ireland. In May 1171, Diarmait died suddenly, and Strongbow, now being in the position to do so, claimed the throne of Leinster for himself. According to Irish law, however, succession to kingship was elective and could only be passed on through the male line of a family; as a result, the claims of the English warlord were rejected by Diarmait's large family. Only one member of the family, Diarmait's son Domnall (c.1140–1175), backed Strongbow.

Soon after Diarmait's death, the Kingdom of Leinster joined the anti-English alliance and Strongbow's military forces came under attack both from within Leinster and from outside the realm. Waterford was invested and Dublin became a target of the Irish counteroffensive. A large Irish army, comprising contingents coming from every corner of the island, surrounded Dublin and operated in combination with a fleet of 30 warships that blockaded the city's bay. Part of the English garrison in Wexford went to Dublin in order to reinforce the local defenders, but the Irish princes used this move to their advantage, launching a rapid attack against Wexford and conquering it while its garrison was smaller than usual. Dublin was besieged for two months: several skirmishes took place, but the Irish warriors never attempted to assault the city, instead planning to starve it into surrender. Having lost Waterford and Wexford and with Dublin under siege, Strongbow agreed to negotiate with his enemies. The peace talks, however, were only tolerated by the English to gain some time; they had no intention of renouncing all the territories they had conquered in Ireland. Before the diplomatic meetings were over, the English garrison of Dublin organised a surprise attack against the Irish camp with great success. Hundreds of Irish warriors were killed, and the siege of Dublin was all but broken. Following this defeat, the Irish troops withdrew from the surroundings of Dublin. The English presence in Ireland was, by now, strong enough that it was very difficult for the local princes to expel the foreign invaders decisively.

Henry II feared that Strongbow could set up an independent kingdom in Ireland, which could dominate the commercial routes crossing the Irish Sea. The English invasion had started as a sort of 'private enterprise', organised in

Infantryman armed with spear and throwing javelin. (Milites Pagenses)

support of the Kingdom of Leinster; now that the alliance between England and Leinster was no longer in existence, Henry II wanted to use Strongbow's footholds on the island in order to conquer a large portion of Ireland. In 1171, he ordered that all of his subjects fighting in Ireland should return home; if they refused to do so, all their possessions would be seized by the Crown. Strongbow, having no choice, responded to this move by stating that all the conquests he had made were at the disposal of the monarchy. Having brought Strongbow back under his personal control, Henry II made him the 'Royal Constable in Ireland' and granted him most of the territories that he had conquered in the previous years. In September 1171, the English monarch finally decided to organise a royal expedition to Ireland. He landed a few weeks later at Waterford, with a large army that comprised 500 knights and 4,000 other soldiers. This was the first time a King of England landed on Irish soil, an event that would be of enormous importance for the history of the British Isles. The English troops marched to Dublin, where they joined forces with the local garrison; here, Henry II assumed formal control over all the Irish lands that were still in English hands. Dublin, Waterford and Wexford were made 'Crown lands' while the Kingdom of Leinster was formally assigned to Strongbow, who was to rule it as a fiefdom of England. A portion of these possessions still had to be reconquered, but Henry II was sure of his final victory. Some minor Irish princes were impressed by the military resources at the disposal of the foreign king and decided to submit without fighting, in order to avoid the invasion of their realms. The King of Connacht, who also had the important honorific title of 'High King of Ireland', did not submit and another two Irish monarchs did the same.

The Irish Church submitted to Henry II, hoping that the arrival of the English would bring peace and political stability to their country. The English monarch organised a synod at Cashel, during which he was recognised by the bishops of Ireland as their temporal overlord. In this political and religious process, Henry II was supported by Pope Alexander III, who considered the submission of the Irish bishops to the English Crown as the first step to impose the Gregorian Reforms over the clergy of Ireland. The Irish clergy had never paid Rome the sums expected by the papacy, but with the English conquests of Henry II, new monastic communities

Infantryman wearing a 'cervelliere' helmet (hemispherical, close-fitting skull cap of steel or iron) and armed with mace. (Les Guerriers du Moyen-Age)

and military orders under the direct control of the papacy were introduced into Ireland. In April 1172, without having seen much action, Henry II returned to England. He left behind some of the most warlike English nobles, such as Hugh de Lacy (before 1135–25 July 1186) and most of his royal troops. In early 1173, however, most of the English barons operating in Ireland abandoned the island to fight for Henry II in the Great Revolt of 1173–1174 (discussed below). With the departure of the king and with the subsequent outbreak of a new civil war in England, the English barons in Ireland limited themselves to launching some incursions against the Irish kingdoms that had not accepted Henry II as their ruler. Dublin, Waterford and Wexford continued to be the main operational bases of the English, with the most important military leader being Strongbow. In 1174, however, Strongbow suffered a significant defeat at the Battle of Thurles, which was won by the new High King of Ireland, Ruaidrí Ua Conchobair (c.1116–2 December 1198). Following this clash, and seeing that the English military presence in Ireland had been notably reduced, the Irish princes, who had been subdued by the English, rose up in revolt and joined the existing anti-Strongbow coalition. Dublin was besieged again, but luckily for the English, a large relief expedition arrived before the Irish could win. In 1175, following some raiding operations organised by the English that had devastating effects, Henry II and the High King of Ireland decided to come to terms and to sign the Treaty of Windsor. This divided Ireland into two spheres of influence: Henry II continued to rule over the lands that had been conquered during the previous years, while the High King of Ireland obtained control over the rest of the island. In 1176, Strongbow died, and in 1177, the English possessions in

Infantryman armed with single-handed falchion. (Les Guerriers du Moyen-Age)

Ireland were organised into the 'Lordship of Ireland'. According to Henry II's plans, the lordship would be given to his son John when he came of age. In the following years, the Treaty of Windsor fell by the wayside and the English nobles in Ireland attacked the Irish kingdoms of Desmond, Thomond and Connacht with the objective of expanding the Lordship of Ireland.

While these events took place in Ireland, since 1173, Henry II had also been facing the so-called 'Great Revolt': this was a civil conflict that almost destroyed the unity of the Angevin Empire and took place in several different areas of Europe. Henry II's first son, commonly known as Young Henry, had already been crowned as his father's successor but was very unhappy with his personal role. He played no role in the government of his future kingdom and was always kept short of money by the ruling monarch. Geoffrey, Duke of Brittany, was also unhappy with his father's political decisions, as was Richard; the latter was strongly supported by his mother Eleanor of Aquitaine, who wished for Richard to be king and whose relationship with Henry II had by now completely disintegrated. Understanding that three of the king's sons and his wife were now against the policies of the Crown, many English barons decided to organise a revolt, hoping to depose Henry II and replace him with Young Henry. When the ruling king gave his youngest son John three important castles belonging to Young Henry, the latter left England and went to Paris under the protection of Louis VII. He was soon followed by his brothers Richard and Geoffrey. Eleanor also tried to go to Paris but was captured by her husband's men before being able to do so. Young Henry could count on the decisive support of Louis – since he promised to cede several portions of his father's French possessions to the French nobles if they supported him against Henry II – and also the new King of Scotland, William I (c.1142–4 December 1214). In just a few months, all the major barons of the Angevin Empire were convinced to revolt against their king, with only Normandy and Anjou remaining loyal to the ruling monarch. In May 1173, Louis VII and Young Henry attempted a pincer movement against Normandy, but this failed completely as Henry II was able to mount a devastating counter-offensive. Following this success, the royalist troops crushed the rebels of Brittany and brought the region back under the control of Henry II.

Infantryman armed with double-handed falchion. (Les Guerriers du Moyen-Age)

In the British Isles, the king was able to stop and defeat a Scottish invasion of Northern England in the summer of 1173 but soon had to face a new menace: Robert de Beaumont (1121–1190), Earl of Leicester, the leader of the revolting English barons, who disembarked in Suffolk alongside 3,000 Flemish mercenaries. This force, however, was crushed by a royal army during the Battle of Fornham (17 October 1173), which saw the capture of the Earl of Leicester and other rebel nobles. In 1174, there was a second Scottish invasion of Northern England, which ended in failure as the attackers were not able to occupy the necessary strategic castles that remained loyal to Henry II. Some months later, the Count of Flanders, who had joined the coalition guided by Young Henry and Louis VII, sent a minor military force to East Anglia and started organising a larger invasion of England. The king was forced to leave Normandy again in order to defend England but was able to expel the Flemish forces from his realm; meanwhile, in France, Louis VII and his son Philip Augustus obtained some victories in Normandy and managed to reach Rouen. However, after restoring the situation in England, Henry II returned to France and reconquered that portion of Normandy. As the revolts in the Angevin Empire had all been crushed and Normandy seemed impossible to conquer, Louis VII had no choice but to come to terms with Henry II. The King of England restored the status quo: Young Henry agreed to cede the disputed English castles to his brother John (who had remained loyal to his father) but in exchange received two castles in Normandy. Richard and Geoffrey were granted half the revenues from Aquitaine and Brittany, respectively. Eleanor of Aquitaine was kept under house arrest, since the king considered her as the real 'brains' of the Great Revolt. William of Scotland was forced to cede five important castles while Philip of Flanders was obliged to assume a neutral position for the years to come. By the end of 1174, Henry II was at the peak of his personal power; his relationship with Louis VII of France, however, remained very complicated.

In 1177, Henry II made John 'Lord of Ireland', as planned some years before, and in 1179 he gave the Duchy of Aquitaine to Richard; two years later, in 1181, Geoffrey finally became Duke of Brittany after marrying Constance, the daughter of his predecessor. Meanwhile, Young Henry spent his time travelling across Europe without playing a significant role in the government of his father. In 1182, having understood that John was the favourite of the king, he reiterated his previous demands that had caused the outbreak of the Great Revolt: like his brothers, he wanted to be granted a portion of the Angevin Empire – most notably the Duchy of Normandy – and wanted the necessary sums of money to support himself with royal dignity. Henry II rejected these requests, as he had done previously, but agreed to increase his eldest son's allowances. Over time, it became clear that tension was rising again in the Angevin Empire; to placate his first son, Henry II asked Richard and Geoffrey to give homage to Young Henry for their lands. The heir to the English throne, however, refused to accept the formal submission of Richard. He wanted to expel his brother from Aquitaine and thus formed an alliance with some of the barons from the region who were unhappy with Richard's rule. Geoffrey sided with Young Henry and provided him an army of Breton mercenaries. In 1183, war broke out between Henry II's sons; the king sided with Richard and fought with him in Aquitaine. After a few months, before either side could win a decisive battle, Young Henry caught a fever and died. At this point, Henry II had to rearrange the plans for his succession and redistribute the lands of the Angevin Empire among his surviving sons. Richard was to become the new King of England and Duke of Normandy, Geoffrey would retain Brittany and John would be given Aquitaine. Richard, however, refused to give up Aquitaine and disobeyed his father. At this point, Geoffrey and John attacked the contested duchy on behalf of their father; a short war began, which ended in stalemate a few months later. During 1185, also thanks to the intervention of Eleanor of Aquitaine, Richard made peace with his father and finally handed over Aquitaine. In that same year, John, who was to rule over Ireland, organised an expedition to the island. This was not a great success, and the English prince achieved little more than building some new castles. In 1186, Geoffrey died during a tournament, and Henry II's succession plans changed once again.

In 1180, Louis VII, personal enemy of Henry II, died, and was replaced on the throne by his ambitious son, Philip Augustus. Philip was strongly determined to destroy the Angevin Empire and was ready to use the frictions existing inside the English royal family to his advantage. In 1186, the French monarch asked Henry II's permission to have custody of Geoffrey's children, and of the Duchy of Brittany, wanting to expel the Angevins from the French fiefdom. If the King of England rejected Philip's request, the French military forces were ready to attack Normandy. Since no agreement was found, both sides mobilised their troops and an indecisive clash took place before the intervention of Pope Urban III (died 20 October 1187), who sponsored a truce. During the ensuing negotiations, the King of France tried to convince Richard to join his cause, but with little success. In that particular moment, Richard deemed Henry II still too strong to be defeated, and furthermore, during 1187, the holy city of Jerusalem was conquered by Saladin (c.1137–4 March 1193) and calls for a new crusade swept Europe. Richard was enthusiastic about the idea of organising a crusade, while both Henry II and Philip Augustus had no interest in wasting their time in what they considered a futile military enterprise. Richard, as 'junior monarch' of England, started to raise taxes and make plans for the expedition to the Holy Land, but his preparations were opposed by his father. Richard also stabilised his position in Aquitaine, attacking Raymond of Toulouse, who was a loyal ally of Philip Augustus. Richard's military initiative, which had not been authorised by his father, led to the outbreak of a new conflict between the Angevin Empire and France. Henry II wanted to avoid a new large-scale conflict with Philip and thus tried to convince

Miniature from the folio 10 recto of the Morgan Bible, representing a battle taking place in front of the walls of a fortified city. The infantryman with glaive (a single-edged blade on the end of a pole) on the left is wearing a padded aketon painted red, while the one with a poleaxe on the right has a light brown aketon. Both have a chapel de fer helmet. (Public domain, The Morgan Library and Museum)

the French king to agree to a long-term peace deal. The young monarch rejected the offer and hostilities commenced, albeit with low intensity. Meanwhile, the relationship between Henry II and Richard further dissolved when the son accused the father of being against the crusade that he was organising.

In 1188, Richard abandoned his father and joined Philip Augustus, giving formal homage to the latter as Duke of Normandy. Following this event, having the main objective of freeing the Holy Land, the papacy intervened again and a new peace conference was organised in 1189. By that time, however, Henry II was suffering from a severe bleeding ulcer and his health was deteriorating very rapidly. The peace talks achieved very little, as the English monarch showed his intention to cede his main possessions to John and not to Richard as agreed previously. After the diplomatic meetings ended, Philip and Richard launched a surprise attack against Henry II's forces in France. The King of England had no choice but to retreat to Normandy, where he was prepared to face an enemy offensive. During most of his life, the Angevin monarch had been a great military leader and in this campaign, which was to be his last, he showed his capabilities to their fullest extent. Instead of defending the borders of Normandy, as expected by his opponents, he turned south towards Anjou to launch a counteroffensive. Here, however, the condition of his health worsened rapidly; before he could die, the king was visited by Richard. Father and son had a last meeting, during which some sort of reconciliation took place between the two, and Richard was designated as the future King of England once again. Shortly after having been informed that his favourite son John had also sided with Richard and Philip, Henry II died in Chinon on 6 July 1189. He remains one of the greatest monarchs in the history of Medieval Europe.

Above left: Peasant infantryman. The foot soldiers of the feudal levies did not wear any form of personal protection, except for a shield and sometimes a simple helmet. (Les Guerriers du Moyen-Age)

Above right: Peasant infantryman. (Les Guerriers du Moyen-Age)

Chapter 6
The Reign of Richard the Lionheart
1189–1199

Richard I, probably the most famous monarch in the history of England, was officially invested as Duke of Normandy a few days after the death of his father; on 3 September 1189, he was crowned King of England in Westminster Abbey. After having spent just a few months in England to stabilise his political position, Richard resumed his military preparations for the long-awaited crusade.

Reconquering Jerusalem had become an obsession for most of Europe's inhabitants, including the King of England; by fighting in the Holy Land, Richard hoped to gain some glory for himself after being overshadowed by his father for many years. Philip Augustus of France, who had been an ally of Richard during the last phase of Henry II's long reign, now feared that the new English king could become too popular in France following his crusade. In 1188, Philip had officially promised to participate to the liberation of Jerusalem, and his failure to do so threatened to severely impact his reputation as a 'pious' monarch. After analysing the situation, Philip Augustus agreed to go on the Third Crusade with Richard. Frederick Redbeard (c.1123–10 June 1190), Holy Roman Emperor and enemy of the Church, joined the kings of England and France. Richard, unlike Philip, was full of religious zeal, spending most his father's treasury and raising taxes to finance the organisation of the crusade. He even agreed to free King William I of Scotland from his oath of loyalty to the King of England in exchange for a payment of 10,000 marks. To raise more funds, the monarch sold rights to public positions and lands to people who were interested in them. Those royal officials who already had important roles in the administration had to pay large sums of money in order to retain them. Before leaving Europe, Richard replaced the local administrators of his French domains with new officials who were loyal to him, and left some of his troops in France in order to protect his possessions from attacks. In the summer of 1190, Richard the Lionheart finally set out on the crusade.

Peasant infantryman. The foot soldiers of the feudal levies used polearms that derived from the working tools of the contemporary peasants, like the one shown here. (Les Guerriers du Moyen-Age)

In September 1190, both Richard and Philip arrived in Sicily; the island was the most prosperous region of the Kingdom of Sicily, founded in 1130 and comprising most of southern Italy. The Italian realm was governed by a Norman royal family and thus its aristocracy had important ties with the English one. In 1189, King William II of Sicily (December 1153–11 November 1189) had died and southern Italy had seen the beginning of a civil war fought between two pretenders to the throne: on one side there was Tancred (1138–20 February 1194), cousin of the defunct monarch, who seized power in Sicily thanks to the support of his warlike aristocracy; on the other side, there was William II's aunt Constance (2 November 1154–27 November 1198), wife of the Holy Roman Emperor Henry VI (November 1165–28 September 1197), son of Frederick Redbeard, who had died on his way to the Holy Land, and legal heir of the defunct King of Sicily. After taking power, Tancred had imprisoned William II's widow, Queen Joan, who was Richard's sister, and refused to give her the money she had inherited according to William's will. When Richard landed in Sicily, at the port city of Messina, the most important logistical base of the crusaders, he demanded the liberation of his sister and required

Miniature from the folio 18 recto of the Morgan Bible, depicting the standard clothes worn by peasants during the 13th century. These were used, with no alterations, by the feudal infantrymen mobilised for war, who had a very humble appearance. The white 'infulae' (a sort of skull cap, with two flaps for the ears) and the wicker wide-brimmed hats were quite popular, as well as the trousers covering legs. The second figure from the left is wearing his white working breeches without the coloured trousers. (Public domain, The Morgan Library and Museum)

the immediate payment of her inheritance. On 28 September, Tancred released Joan but did not pay the sum that Richard requested. The presence of many English and French soldiers in Sicily added confusion to the ongoing political struggles that ravaged the Kingdom of Sicily; the local population of the island perceived the strangers as a potential menace and jealous of the realm's independence. In October, the people of Messina rose up against the crusaders and demanded the foreigners leave their land. Richard, in order to show his military superiority to both Tancred and Philip, who were near Messina, attacked the city and conquered it on 4 October 1190. After looting and burning Messina, Richard the Lionheart transformed the Sicilian port into his main military base. On 4 March, after several months of increasing tensions, and thanks to the mediation of Philip, a treaty was signed between Richard and Tancred. According to this, Joan was to receive 20,000 ounces of gold as compensation for her inheritance.

Peasant infantryman of the feudal levy. (Les Seigneurs d'Orient)

After these events, both Richard and Philip remained in Sicily in order to complete their preparations before sailing to the Holy Land. During this period, however, tension increased between the two monarchs, despite being 'allies' (at least on paper). Frequent skirmishes took place between the English and French soldiers, while Philip Augustus started plotting with Tancred. In the end, however, open hostilities were avoided and both monarchs left southern Italy in the spring of 1191. Richard's crusader fleet was dispersed by a storm during the ensuing journey, and some of the king's ships, including those transporting his sister Joan and his promised wife Berengaria of Navarre (c.1170–23 December 1230), were forced to dock in Cyprus due to bad weather conditions. Once on the island, the two ladies were captured by the local ruler Isaac Comnenos (c. 1155–1195/1196). In May, Richard arrived in Cyprus at the head of his military forces and ordered Isaac to release his English prisoners and give his treasure to the crusaders. The ruler of Cyprus refused, so Richard took the important city of Limassol in retaliation. All the crusade leaders who were in Cyprus supported the Lionheart, as well as some local magnates who were already against Isaac Comnenos. As a result, by the beginning of July, the King of England had been able to conquer the whole island of Cyprus and capture Isaac. The occupation of Cyprus had a great strategic importance, since its ports could now act as naval bases for the crusaders. After selling his newly conquered territories to the Knights Templar, Richard the Lionheart left Cyprus for Acre on 5 June. Before leaving Limassol, on the southern coast of Cyprus, he married Berengaria, the heir of the Spanish Kingdom of Navarre, which bordered the southern part of Aquitaine and was of great strategic importance for Richard.

On 9 October 1192, after more than a year spent fighting in the Holy Land, Richard the Lionheart decided to return to England. In the Kingdom of Jerusalem, he had shown all his valour and had defeated the Islamic forces on several occasions, but he had not been able to change the political situation in the Levant as he had hoped. A fragile peace was concluded with Saladin, but the most important questions remained unresolved. In the Holy Land, the Lionheart had to face the hostility of the other crusader leaders, who saw his participation to the Third Crusade as a threat to their expansionist ambitions in the Levant. The rivalry between Richard and Philip Augustus grew even stronger and would soon cause the outbreak of new hostilities in Europe. Moreover, Richard's return journey to England did not go as planned: bad weather forced him to stop at Corfu, a Greek island that was part of the Byzantine Empire, which was dominated by Emperor Isaac II Angelos (September 1156–January 1204), who was still furious with Richard for his occupation of Cyprus, which had always been part of the Byzantine possessions. In order to avoid capture on Byzantine land, the King of England was forced to sail from Corfu disguised as a normal knight and with just four attendants. The ship transporting him, however, was wrecked near Aquileia in northeastern Italy. At this point, Richard was forced to continue his journey by following a dangerous land route that crossed the lands of central Europe dominated by the Holy Roman Empire. Shortly before December, not far from Vienna, Richard was captured by the men of Leopold V of Austria (1157–31 December 1194). Leopold had participated in the Third Crusade like the Lionheart and had been one of its main leaders together with the monarchs of England and France. In the Kingdom of Jerusalem, Richard and Leopold had supported two different candidates to the local throne and the King of England had even humiliated Leopold by casting down his standard from the walls of Acre. The imprisonment of Richard had no real legal basis and was the result of a personal vendetta of Leopold; in fact, the latter, was excommunicated by the Pope for his actions. In March 1193, Richard was handed over to Henry VI, Holy Roman Emperor, who imprisoned him in one of his castles. Henry was furious with the king because he had recognised Tancred as King of Sicily during his stay in southern Italy instead of supporting the claims of his wife, Constance. The Holy Roman Emperor was organising a large military expedition with the objective of conquering the Kingdom of Sicily, and needed a lot of money. As a result, he decided to hold the King of England to ransom and demanded 150,000 marks for his liberation. This was a very large sum for the time, corresponding to two or three times the annual income of the English Crown. Eleanor of Aquitaine started working to raise the 150,000 marks, taxing clergy and laymen for a quarter of the value of their properties. The treasures of the churches were confiscated and some extra money was raised from ordinary taxes. Before leaving England for the Holy Land, Richard had tried to secure for himself the loyalty of his brother John by giving him some of the richest English counties (Cornwall, Derby, Devon, Dorset, Nottingham and Somerset). During the Lionheart's absence, however, John started to act as a king: he created an independent royal court and began nurturing dangerous ambitions. Firstly, he wanted to replace William de Longchamp (died 1197), who had been nominated chancellor by his brother; secondly, he wanted to be recognised as the future monarch of England. After some weeks of growing tensions, armed conflict broke out between John and Longchamp; by October 1191, the latter had been defeated and John controlled most of the realm. John could count on the support of several nobles as well as of the population of London, since he had made great promises to the inhabitants of the city. By now, Richard was already in Cyprus, but he was

Above left: Peasant infantryman armed with wooden mace. (Milites Pagenses)

Above right: Peasant infantryman armed with flail, which was an agricultural tool used for separating grains from their husks. (Les Guerriers du Moyen-Age)

able to organise a counteroffensive against his brother from a distance: he sent Walter of Coutances (died 16 November 1207), the Archbishop of Rouen, to England with the precise task of restoring order. A new phase of political turmoil started during which John began exploring the possibility of an alliance with Philip Augustus, who returned from the crusade before Richard. After the Lionheart was captured in Austria, John began asserting that his brother was dead in order to be crowned as his heir; this attempt, however, failed miserably. He went to Paris, where he allied himself with the King of France; John agreed to set aside his wife, Isabella of Gloucester (c.1174–14 October 1217), and to marry Philip's sister Alys. Together, John and Philip offered 80,000 marks to Henry VI to hold Richard prisoner for several years. The Holy Roman Emperor, however, turned down the offer, as he wanted to be paid the 150,000 initially requested. Finally, thanks to the great efforts of Eleanor of Aquitaine, the ransom was paid and, on 4 February 1194, Richard was freed. During the previous months, fighting had taken place in England between John's supporters and the royalists, but the latter had experienced no difficulties in keeping the situation under control. The famous stories of Robin Hood and of Ivanhoe are set during this historical period, one of the most controversial of Plantagenet England. With the Lionheart's return to England, John's supporters surrendered and their leader retreated to Normandy. Richard did not punish his younger brother particularly severely; he did not order his imprisonment but simply removed him from all his land possessions in England.

After having restored order in his kingdom, the Lionheart went to France in order to fight against Philip Augustus. The latter had attacked Normandy during Richard's captivity and had occupied the region of Vexin. Richard spent the following years building new castles in Normandy and skirmishing with the French troops; at the same time, he organised a large alliance against his rival Philip Augustus that comprised Baldwin IX (1172–1205), Count of Flanders, and Sancho VI (died 27 June 1194), King of Navarre. On the field, the Angevin forces obtained several victories over the French. Philip was defeated for the first time at the Battle of Fréteval in 1194 and later at the larger Battle of Gisors in 1198. The latter saw the clash between 200 English knights and 300 French ones, and was decided by an audacious charge led by the Lionheart. In March 1199, Richard moved to Limousin, in order to suppress a revolt of the local ruler Aimar V of Limoges (c.1135–c.1199). The Lionheart was struggling to keep the Angevin Empire, inherited from his father, united and had understood that Philip Augustus' main target was the Duchy of Normandy: as a result, he employed all his material resources and personal energy to secure his position in northern France. On 26 March, while besieging a castle in Limousin, the Lionheart was hit in the shoulder by the dart of a crossbow. The wound, which seemed curable at the beginning, turned gangrenous very rapidly. On 6 April 1199, in the arms of his mother Eleanor of Aquitaine, Richard the Lionheart died. Since the king had no legitimate heirs, he was succeeded by his brother John as monarch of England. The French territories of the Angevins rejected John's rule, an act that marked the beginning of the end for the empire created by Henry II.

Chapter 7
The Reign of King John 1199–1216

Upon Richard's death, there were two potential claimants to the English throne: John, or the young Arthur I of Brittany (29 March 1187–c.1203), who was the son of John's elder brother, Geoffrey. John, however, was supported by most of the English aristocrats and was backed by his mother Eleanor of Aquitaine: consequently, he was crowned in Westminster soon after the death of his brother. Arthur was supported by the nobles of Brittany, Maine and Anjou; in addition, he had an ally in Philip Augustus, who was now determined to continue his campaigns in Normandy against the new English monarch. Soon after becoming king, John had to defend the Duchy of Normandy from the assaults of Arthur and Philip. He could count on the excellent castles that had been built by his brother as well as on the network of regional alliances that had been created by the Lionheart. Since neither side was able to gain the upper hand in the hostilities, in January 1200 John and Philip met to negotiate the terms for peace (under strong pressure from the papacy). The Treaty of Le Goulet was signed some months later, according to which Philip recognised John as the legitimate heir of Richard's French possessions, and John recognised Philip as his feudal overlord in France. The new peace, however, was very short-lived, and in 1202 both sides resumed the hostilities. At the beginning of the new war, the King of England adopted a defensive attitude similar to that of 1199: he avoided a pitched battle against the French and limited himself to defending his strong castles. Furthermore, on this occasion, Normandy was being attacked by two armies, the French one of Philip Augustus and the Breton one of Arthur. After some indecisive engagements, John decided to face Arthur on the open field and defeated him at the Battle of Mirebeau on 31 July 1202; this was the first important victory for the King of England, since he was able to capture Arthur and most of his supporters. The young Duke of Brittany would be killed some months later, in order to eliminate a dangerous potential rival for John. At this point in the war, however, John started to experience some serious difficulties: since his armies were mostly made up of mercenaries recruited from Flanders and from Brabant, his financial resources were becoming increasingly smaller. In addition, he was not able to secure his control over the territories that had supported Arthur.

Peasant infantryman equipped with a two-handed falchion. (Les Guerriers du Moyen-Age)

As time went on, an increasing number of Angevin nobles, who had been loyal to Richard the Lionheart, started to abandon John. With Arthur's death and with the King of England experiencing serious military difficulties, the nobles began to see Philip Augustus as their possible new ruler. By this time, the King of France was besieging Chateau Gaillard, the strongest fortification built by Richard the Lionheart to defend the borders of Normandy; John attempted to relieve the besieged garrison in the late months of 1203, but his counteroffensive failed. The frustrated English monarch then moved to Brittany, where the local population had started revolting against him. John crushed the Breton revolt with great determination, but could do very little to improve his general military situation; Philip Augustus, who could count on large feudal military forces, was gradually gaining the upper hand. In March 1204, after a long and complex siege, Chateau Gaillard was conquered by the French, and some weeks after this important event, Eleanor of Aquitaine died. John's forces in Normandy tried to establish a new defensive line after the fall of their main stronghold, but Philip Augustus was able to move around the enemy defences and launch a devastating offensive against the very heart of Normandy without meeting significant resistance. By August 1204, the King of France had conquered the whole of Normandy and could continue his advance; he also invaded Anjou and Poitou, which were occupied quite easily by the French thanks to the collaboration of the local nobles. By the end of the year, of the Angevin Empire's French territories only the Duchy of Aquitaine remained in John's hands. The military disasters of 1203–1204 greatly weakened the international position of the King of England, who had to secure the sea route connecting Aquitaine to England following the loss of the land route that crossed Normandy. In addition, John had to secure England against a potential French invasion: he reorganised his feudal military forces in order to have a number of permanent troops at his disposal and built many new warships in order to control the English Channel. His main objective, however, remained reconquering Normandy.

By 1212, King John could count on a large fleet of over 100 military vessels, made up of three main components: royal galleys built during the previous years; smaller warships provided by the coastal centres of the Cinque Ports (Hastings, New Romney, Hythe, Dover and Sandwich); and merchant ships converted to military use. John's new fleet was commanded by William of Wrotham (died c.1217) and had Portsmouth as its main operational base. The new naval resources assembled by John, however, were mostly used for defensive purposes: instead of attempting a landing in Normandy, William of Wrotham was tasked with protecting the southern coast of England from any eventual attack organised by the French. King John wanted to reconquer Normandy by attacking it from the south, and his plan was to raise substantial land forces in Aquitaine and use these to attack the French in Poitou (a key region located north of Aquitaine and south of Normandy). In 1206, the same John went to Poitou to organise the first offensive of this kind, but he was forced to fight a minor campaign on the southern border of Aquitaine against Alfonso VIII of Castile (11 November 1155–5 October 1214). After losing precious time, the English monarch finally attacked Poitou and took the important city of Angers. When Philip Augustus moved south to intercept John, the campaign ended in stalemate and a truce of two years was reached between the two kings. This brief period of peace was employed by John to gather more financial resources in view of a new attack on Normandy. The English monarch also concluded some important military alliances with Otto IV (1175–19 May 1218), a pretender to the crown of Holy Roman Emperor, and with a few major French aristocrats (Renaud of Boulogne [c.1165–1227] and Ferdinand of Flanders [24 March 1188–27 July 1233], among others). In 1213, Philip Augustus took the initiative before John and sent his elder son, Louis, to invade Flanders: his plan was to take control of the important Flemish ports in order to organise an invasion of England. John was thus forced to use his new fleet for the first time and launched a pre-emptive strike against the French naval forces that were anchored in the harbour of Damme. The English raid was a success and resulted in the destruction of most of Philip's vessels; as a result, the plans for a French invasion of England had to be abandoned.

Archer wearing Phrygian cap. (Milites Pagenses)

France was not the only external enemy of King John, since he also had to fight in Scotland, Wales and Ireland during his reign. In 1209, the English monarch was informed of William I of Scotland's intention to form an alliance with the French; as a result, he decided to invade Scotland and after a very rapid campaign he forced the Scottish monarch to sign the Treaty of Norham. In accordance with the treaty, William I abandoned all his expansionist ambitions over Northern England and paid a large sum of money to King John. In Wales, the English king had to face a major uprising in 1211, which began because of a succession crisis in one of the Welsh princedoms. In order to restore order and to reconfirm English political influence, John mounted a large-scale invasion with success. For the first time, a royal army marched across Wales and reached the very heartland of the Welsh princedoms; soon after the end of the expedition, however, the local warlords regained most of their usual autonomy and thus the situation went back to the status quo. John remained 'Lord of Ireland' for the entire duration of his reign. His Irish policy was very simple: he tried to expand the English territorial possessions in every possible way, with diplomacy or with small military interventions. In 1210, he landed in Ireland at the head of a sizeable army in order to crush a rebellion of the local Anglo-Irish barons who had revolted

Archer of the 11th century. (Historia Aquitanorum)

against his rule. The expedition was a success and order was restored, but John was not able to extend his authority over that part of Ireland, which was still fully independent from England. John did not change the relationships existing between his kingdom and the Celtic nations: the border issues with Scotland remained open despite a temporary success; Wales continued to be a rebellious country enjoying a high degree of political autonomy; and the English positions in Ireland remained precarious.

In 1214, King John organised his last military campaign in Continental Europe, still with the objective of taking Normandy back from Philip Augustus. This time, he had a good chance of victory, since he had been able to organise a very strong anti-French military alliance. Otto IV had finally been proclaimed Holy Roman Emperor by a good number of the German princes and thus was now ready to help his English ally with substantial military resources. Renaud of Boulogne and Ferdinand of Flanders, being extremely worried about their king's ambitions of political centralisation, were also

Archer of the 11th century. (Les Seigneurs d'Orient)

determined to fight on King John's side. The English monarch constructed a very complex military plan. At the head of an army mostly made up of mercenaries, he would attack from Aquitaine by crossing Poitou and would attack the city of Paris; his three allies (Otto, Renaud and Ferdinand) would assemble an army in Flanders and attack the French from the northeast. The allied forces in Flanders would be supported by an English contingent commanded by William Longespée (c.1167–7 March 1226), one of John's most loyal and most experienced military commanders. Initially, everything worked well for King John: moving from Aquitaine, he outmanoeuvred the French forces facing him commanded by Prince Louis of France, and as a result, the English were able to reconquer the County of Anjou by the end of June. Meanwhile, in the north, Philip Augustus had to mobilise his military forces very rapidly in order to face the threat represented by Otto's large army. The two opposing forces met on 27 July, at the plain of Bouvines; here, one of the largest and most important battles of the Middle Ages was fought. Philip Augustus' army consisted of around 1,300 heavy knights (of whom 765 came from the lands of the royal domain) and 300 'mounted sergeants'; these were supported by 3,160 infantrymen provided by the municipalities of northern France, which contributed men to the French war effort according to their demographic and economic capabilities. The King of France could also count on 2,000 mercenary infantrymen, and thus his troops numbered a total of 6,700 men. These were deployed on the field of conflict into battles: the right battle consisted of knights coming from Champagne, Burgundy and Picardy, as well as 150 'mounted sergeants' coming from Soissons; the central battle consisted of the knights coming from the lands of the royal domain, as well as the foot militiamen sent by the towns of northern France; the left battle consisted of Breton knights and of other foot militiamen provided by the municipalities. Behind the French army there was the bridge of Bouvines, the only means of retreat across the marshes, guarded by 150 mounted sergeants. The Imperial army of Otto comprised around 1,500 knights (including 650 coming from Flanders, and 500 coming from Hainaut) plus 7,500 infantrymen (including hundreds of English archers). Like Philip Augustus, the Holy Roman Emperor divided his troops into three battles: the left battle consisted of Flemish knights, supported by foot soldiers coming from Flanders and Hainaut; the central battle consisted of Saxon knights as well as infantrymen coming from Germany and the Brabant (who were equipped with long pikes); and the right battle, which consisted of English knights and foot soldiers from Brabant, was commanded by William Longespée. The English archers were deployed as a 'reserve' on the extreme right flank of the Imperial army. The Battle of Bouvines began with an attack coming from the French right flank, launched by the 150 lightly armoured mounted sergeants against the Flemish knights. This assault was easily repulsed by Otto's men and was followed by a second attack led by the knights of Champagne; this was also stopped by the Flemish knights, who later took the initiative. To stop the Flemish advance, the French had no choice but to launch several frontal charges with all their knights of the left division until the enemy ranks were broken after three hours of bitter fighting. In the centre, the French urban militiamen were easily crushed by Otto's elite German knights; the French monarch, who was in the centre of his line, was unhorsed during this phase of the battle and saved with great difficulty by his knights. The French had to launch several frontal charges with all the available knights until Otto's men were finally pushed back. The Emperor ran the risk of being captured, and his personal banner was taken by the French knights. On the Imperial left, William Longespée, after some initial success, was unhorsed and captured; his soldiers, demoralised, fled from the battlefield after seeing very little action. When the allied forces started to abandon the battlefield, a force of 700 pikemen from Brabant resisted alone against the advancing French by forming a defensive ring. The Imperial infantrymen, led by Reginald of Boulogne, repulsed all the attacks of the French cavalry and gained some precious time for the retreat of their comrades until being completely crushed. The Battle of Bouvines was a splendid victory for Philip Augustus: the enemy army that was invading northern France was completely destroyed along with King John's plans. With no hope of continuing his campaign from Aquitaine with success, the King of England made peace with the King of France: Anjou was returned to Philip and John paid an economic compensation to his rival. The Battle of Bouvines had important consequences also for the political situation of England, as it destroyed all hopes for a restoration of the Angevin Empire. King John's position became extremely precarious in his home realm, and the English barons were ready to take advantage of this situation in order to pursue their own interests.

Like his predecessors Henry II and Richard, John justified his political actions as a king on the basis that he – as a monarch – was above the law since he possessed the quality of 'divine majesty'. This concept was widespread in Europe during the first half of the Middle Ages, but was not necessarily accepted as readily as one might expect. Many intellectuals of the time did not consider the nature of kingship as something 'divine'; they believed, instead, that monarchs should rule in accordance with the custom and the law. In England, this latter vision of royal power was well established by the beginning of the 13th century and supported by most of the important barons. According to this view, the king had to take council with the aristocrats before making any major decision. The personal power of the king was exerted through a sophisticated system of administration, which comprised a series of different 'offices': the Chancery kept written records of all the official communications sent and received by the king; the Treasury dealt with financial income; and the Exchequer dealt with financial expenditure. In addition, there were the judges who administered justice across the kingdom according to their different jurisdictions. Royal courts sometimes played a significant role in local law cases, especially after King John increased the professionalism of his local officials, like the sergeants or the bailiffs, meaning they responded only to the central government and were independent of the powers of the local feudal lords. Before the ascendancy of the new monarch, especially under Richard the Lionheart, local justice had been mostly administered by the feudal lords; as a result, the king's administrative reforms were very unpopular among the aristocrats, who had no intention to renounce part of their personal power. Like Henry II and Richard, John had a peripatetic court that travelled around the realm for most of the year; this was made in order to have direct control of the territories and of the various barons. During his

Crossbowman (left) and archer (right). (Historia Aquitanorum)

reign, King John spent enormous sums of money funding his military expeditions in France; since the English nobles were not willing to fight on his side in Normandy or in Aquitaine, he had to rely – quite substantially – on the use of foreign mercenaries, and this augmented the costs of the war efforts. As discussed, John also had to build a massive military fleet in a very short period, and this had a great impact over the finances of the realm. Like his predecessors, the king could count on three main sources of income to fund his military expeditions: the revenues coming from the lands of the royal domain or 'demesne'; the taxation raised through royal rights from the baronial lands, and the revenues coming from direct taxation. During the first period of his reign, Richard the Lionheart had sold many properties of the royal domain in order to fund the Third Crusade, and thus the general value of the demesne had become less significant than before. Since augmenting the revenues coming from direct taxation was extremely difficult, John had no choice but to introduce new forms of indirect taxation based on feudal rights. The monarch created the so-called 'scutage system', according to which the nobles could avoid military service by sending a cash payment to the king. John also sold some royal feudal rights to his most loyal barons in order to earn some money. Generally speaking, the royal management of taxation was quite arbitrary, since it was heavily influenced by the king's personal attitude towards the individual nobles. Debts owed to the Crown by the aristocrats who supported the monarch could be easily 'forgiven', while those owed by barons who opposed the policy of John were enforced with a certain regularity. Indirect taxation was particularly heavy under King John's reign, and this caused great malcontent among his barons: he levied scutage payments 11 times during his 17 years of rule, something unprecedented in English history. The monarch also maximised his right to demand relief payments when properties of the nobles (including castles) were inherited by their heirs. This was a cause of malcontent, together with the sale of sheriff appointments. The new sheriffs spent large sums of money to 'purchase' their appointments as royal officials and usually made back their investment by increasing fines and penalties on the inhabitants of their territory. The king also sold charters for the creation of new towns and new markets across his realm on a scale never seen before; he even introduced a new tax on income and movable goods during 1207. The lands of the barons who could not pay or refused to pay the new taxes of King John were usually confiscated: as a result, with the progression of time, his economic and financial policy became particularly hated across the realm (especially after it became apparent that the king had no chance of reconquering Normandy).

King John's reign was also characterised by a difficult relationship with the papacy. In 1205, the monarch became involved in a dispute with Pope Innocent III (22 February 1161–16 July 1216) over the choice of the new Archbishop of Canterbury that almost caused the English king's excommunication. During the long struggle between John and the papacy, the Crown confiscated all the properties and the goods of the English clergymen who remained loyal to the Pope. By selling the confiscated monasteries and obtaining control over the treasures of the churches, King John was able to cover most of his military expenses. The controversy with the Pope came to an end in 1213, only when the monarch agreed to recognise the candidate supported by the papacy as the new legitimate Archbishop of Canterbury; in exchange for this, however, John was to keep all the properties and goods that he had confiscated from the English clergy during the previous years. The living conditions of the poorest subjects, most notably the peasants, were very difficult: a bad harvest, for example, could cause the death of an entire family. John did very little to improve the quality of life of the common people, paying attention only to the requests of London's inhabitants, since the latter could influence the political life of the realm by revolting against the Crown.

Like for his predecessors, John's power was based on his royal household. This included two different groups of people, with different military and administrative functions. The first group was that of the 'familiares regis', who were the relatives or immediate friends of the monarch who followed him around

Archer wearing a peasant headgear made of wicker. (Les Guerriers du Moyen-Age)

the country and were part of the court. Generally speaking, the familiares regis all had important military functions and acted as 'field commanders' in case of war. The second group was that of the 'curia regis', which was made up of senior officials and agents who performed important administrative functions. With the progression of time, an increasing number of 'new men' (nobles of low rank) entered the exclusive circle of the curia regis, while the familiares regis continued to be made up mostly of relatives/personal friends of the monarch. The English barons hated the members of the curia regis because the latter were more powerful than the fomer but came from an inferior social class; in addition, many of these officials were experienced mercenaries coming from France and not subjects of the English Crown. By reforming taxation and justice according to his own needs, King John created a new system of power that could easily destroy any baron who opposed his rule. The monarch had a very negative opinion of most of his nobles, fearing that they may revolt against him, and preferred to follow the advice of his 'new men' instead of consulting the aristocrats before taking important decisions. When a baron was suspected of treason, he soon became the target of the king's 'malevolentia' or 'bad will': he could be easily exiled or killed, without any real juridical justification. As a result of all the political, administrative and economical reforms introduced by King John the English barons started to organise a major uprising against the Crown in the hope of removing the hated monarch. Their plans began in earnest soon after the Battle of Bouvines. On the understanding that the French territories of the Angevin Empire had been lost forever (with the exception of Aquitaine) and that they could count on the direct support of Philip Augustus, the barons initiated their revolt. Before this could could start, King John was to hold a council in London during January 1215 to discuss some potential reforms; meanwhile, however, he also began recruiting mercenaries from France.

After the talks came to nothing, in May 1215 the barons congregated at Northampton and officially renounced their feudal ties to King John. Robert Fitzwalter (died 9 December 1235) was chosen as their military leader. The troops assembled by the English aristocrats were collectively known as the 'Army of

Right: Archer equipped with cevelliere helmet and padded aketon. (Les Guerriers du Moyen-Age)

Below: Miniature from the folio 23 verso of the Morgan Bible, showing the culminant moment of a siege. The attackers are employing a trebuchet, while the defenders include an archer armed with a longbow and equipped with a simple skull helmet (cevelliere). (Public domain, The Morgan Library and Museum)

God', since the barons were sure of fighting in the name of a superior moral authority. They marched on London and easily took the capital, as well as the important cities of Lincoln and Exeter. In this initial phase of the famous 'First Barons' War', the monarch tried to find a compromise with the revolting nobles, as he was weak militarily. He had a meeting with the rebel leaders in June 1215, not far from Windsor: the two sides agreed to create a charter that would contain the political requests of the barons. This document, which was later renamed 'Magna Carta' or 'Great Charter', contained a wide proposal for political reform: it promised protection of church rights, protection from illegal imprisonment, access to swift justice, balanced taxation applied only with baronial consent, and limitations on the indirect forms of feudal taxation (most notably on the scutage system). In practice, the Great Charter was a form of 'proto-constitution' created according to the mentality of the Middle Ages. A council of 25 barons was formed to monitor King John's adherence to the document, but the Army of God would be disbanded and the city of London returned to the monarch. However, since the king appeared to have no real intention of implementing the peace agreement that had been reached with the nobles, the barons did not demobilise their military forces and did not surrender London. At this point, it became clear that both sides were ready to fight. John appealed to Pope Innocent III for help and the latter excommunicated the rebel barons after declaring that the Magna Carta contained illegal and unjust requests.

By the time fighting began, King John, despite the numerical superiority of his enemies, was well prepared for war: he had recruited a substantial number of mercenaries and could count on the support of the powerful Marcher Lords. In addition, the monarch controlled a network of strong royal castles and still had large financial resources at his disposal. The monarch's strategy was very simple: isolating and defeating the Army of God in London before the King of France could land his troops in Southern England. Unsurprisingly, Philip Augustus and his young son Louis supported the English barons from the beginning of their rebellion. The revolt of the barons exposed England also to other external threats: in the northern portion of Wales, a new rebellion broke out and Alexander II of Scotland crossed the northern border to support the rebels. King John reacted rapidly to these events, taking the castle of Rochester from the barons in order to regain control over the southeastern route to London. He then sent William Longespée (who had been freed) to retake the north-western route to the capital and moved north with most of his forces to

Crossbowman of the 11th century. (Historia Aquitanorum).

ravage the lands of the local barons and deal with Alexander II. King John's campaign in the north was a real success: he defeated the barons and reconquered most of Northern England, pushing the Scottish troops back to Edinburgh. At this point, understanding that defeat was near for them, the English nobles invited Louis of France to guide them. Philip Augustus' son had the intention to land in the south of England in May 1216, and thus John sent his powerful fleet to intercept him: unluckily for the king, however, a series of storms dispersed his warships, enabling the French to land unopposed in Kent. The region was conquered quite easily by Louis, including the important royal castles of Canterbury and Rochester. On 25 July, the Anglo-French forces of the barons moved to the key castle of Dover, which was well supplied and had a large garrison. The siege of the stronghold lasted for three months, but in the end Louis was forced to abandon it in order to move on London. In addition to that of Dover, the castles of Windsor and Lincoln also resisted the besieging operations of the Anglo-French forces. When a pitched battle between John and Louis seemed imminent, Alexander II invaded Northern England again and the royal army had to move north in order to intercept the Scottish forces (which had already occupied Carlisle). Being unable to crush the invading Alexander II or occupy London before the arrival of Louis, the king fell back to Winchester where he started reorganising his forces.

Crossbowman equipped with cervelliere helmet and padded aketon. (Les Guerriers du Moyen-Age)

The French prince entered London after encountering very little resistance and was soon proclaimed (though not crowned) King of England. Alexander II was present at the coronation ceremony and gave homage to Louis, since he had important fiefs in England. With the progression of time, however, many barons started to change their attitude towards their foreign ally: initially they had invited the French because they wanted to defeat John, but now England was running the risk of becoming a domain of Philip Augustus. Some very important nobles who had previously abandoned King John, like William Longespée, changed side and joined the royalists. Despite the defection of some aristocrats who had initially supported him, Louis continued his conquest of England: he advanced westwards and besieged the castle of Winchester. This was conquered after ten days of fighting, but King John had already abandoned it. In September 1216, John launched a strong counteroffensive: he attacked eastwards between London and Cambridge, in order to break up the positions of his enemies. While leading the offensive, however, the monarch contracted dysentery and fell ill. On 19 October 1216,

Above left: Crossbowman wearing cervelliere helmet. (Les Guerriers du Moyen-Age)

Above right: Crossbowman recharging his weapon. (Les Guerriers du Moyen-Age)

the king died at the castle of Newark, in Nottinghamshire. With his death, the main reason behind the outbreak of the ongoing conflict ceased to exist. The barons, having reached their objective without fighting a single pitched battle, now decided to expel the French from their territories, as well as Louis. Prince Henry, the son and heir of King John (1 October 1207–16 November 1272), was a child of nine years and thus was not perceived as a menace like the foreign prince. Most of the barons abandoned their former French allies and crowned the young Henry III in Gloucester Abbey. Louis still controlled London and a good portion of England, but his forces were now at a clear numerical disadvantage.

Chapter 8
The Reign of Henry III
1216–1272

On 12 November 1216, the Magna Carta was officially re-issued in the name of the new monarch, Henry III. The revised version of the original charter was sealed by the baron who had been made regent of the infant king, William Marshal (c.1147–14 May 1219). Slowly managed to get most barons to abandon Louis, but the civil war between the royalists and the foreign pretender to the throne lasted for another year. During the last weeks of 1216, Louis occupied some important castles, but in early 1217 he decided to return to his father's kingdom in search of some fresh reinforcements. To reach France, he had to cross the regions of Sussex and Kent, where a strong resistance movement had gradually developed: he was attacked on several occasions during his journey and was ambushed at Lewes. Louis lost many of his men during these minor clashes, but before he could leave England a new French fleet, with reinforcements and supplies, arrived. Now that the barons were his new enemies, Louis was becoming increasingly dependent on the reinforcements/supplies sent by his father from France; as a result, he absolutely needed to conquer the port of Dover in order to use it as his main naval base. The French prince besieged the fortifications of Dover for a second time, but on this occasion he was not able to take them. While the French were concentrating their efforts against Dover, William Marshal attacked the military forces of those barons who were still fighting on Louis' side near the castle of Lincoln in May 1217. In what became known as the Second Battle of Lincoln, 1,000 men assembled by William Marshal were able to defeat 1,600 pro-Louis soldiers who were besieging the castle of Lincoln (the garrison that was loyal to Henry III). After the Second Battle of Lincoln, Louis decided to raise his second siege of Dover and went back to London with

**Crossbowman with chapel de fer helmet and chainmail.
(Les Guerriers du Moyen-Age)**

the reinforcements that he had received. Some negotiations between the French prince and William Marshal took place at this point of the war, but they came to nothing and the hostilities continued. Some weeks later, there was a real turn in the tide, as a new French fleet that had been sent to support Louis was defeated by the English warships at the Battle of Sandwich on 24 August 1217. The French fleet was commanded by the famous Eustace the Monk (c.1170–24 August 1217), an adventurer who once belonged to a monastic order before becoming a pirate. During the years 1205–1208, Eustace and his companions worked for King John: the monarch had given the pirate leader the Channel Islands and permitted him to use Winchelsea as his main base in England. In 1212, however, the former monk changed sides and started to serve Philip Augustus. It was thanks to Eustace that Louis landed in Southern England to support the revolting barons, and it was thanks to him that the French conquered the Cinque Ports.

In the late summer of 1217, Philip Augustus sent a new fleet full of reinforcements and supplies to England, commanded by Eustace the Monk. The crew of the English warships built by King John now had a great occasion to show their valour. They were commanded by Hubert de Burgh (c.1170–before 5 May 1243) and had one precise order: crushing the French fleet that was coming from Calais. Initially, the sailors of the Cinque Ports, who had been treated very badly by the defunct King John, had no intention to fight against the French, but in the end they were convinced with the promise of being given great spoils should they destroy them. Eustace the Monk, who was not a French commander from a formal point of view, could count on 11 warships and 70 smaller transport vessels (which carried supplies). The English fleet had 16 warships and 20 smaller auxiliary vessels. When the French armada sailed past Sandwich, the English fleet in the port came out and attacked them. Eustace was trying to reach the estuary of the Thames, since his main objective was to reinforce Louis in London. Soon after the beginning of the clash, the English warships gained the windward position, and this gave them a great advantage. The English combat vessels were smaller than their French equivalents, but each of them had a contingent of archers; these killed many enemy sailors and soldiers from a distance before the French bowmen on Eustace's vessels could respond effectively. After some very hard fighting, the French flagship was boarded by the English and Eustace was captured and later executed as a traitor. Defeated, the remaining French warships returned to Calais. Most of the transport vessels that were full of supplies were captured by the English. The Battle of Sandwich, one of the greatest naval clashes of the Middle Ages, was decisive for determining the outcome of the First Barons' War: after such a defeat, with the English in full control of the Channel, Philip Augustus decided to stop supporting his son. Louis was totally cut off from France and was abandoned by all his remaining English supporters. On 12 September 1217, a peace treaty was signed between the two warring parts at Kingston upon Thames. Louis formally renounced all his claims to the throne of England in return for being allowed to return to his country. Henry III, the new King of England, pardoned all the barons who had remained loyal to the French. England was again united and had avoided foreign occupation; Henry III would now guide the realm with the decisive support of William Marshal.

With the end of the hostilities in 1217, William Marshal faced the task of rebuilding royal authority across large portions of England. The realm was in a state of complete disorder: the network of county sheriffs had collapsed together with the juridical system, unauthorised castles and fortifications had been built everywhere, the raising of taxes had become extremely difficult, and most of the peasants were on the verge of starvation. The Kingdom of Scotland continued to represent a menace for Northern England and the Welsh Marches were threatened by the powerful Welsh leader Llywelyn (c.1173–11 April 1240). Llywelyn was at the head of the Kingdom of Gwynedd, the most important of the Welsh princedoms; in 1211, after revolting against King John, he had been defeated by the English, but during the following years he had been able to restore his power. In 1213, Llywelyn formed an alliance with

Miniature from the folio 42 recto of the Morgan Bible, depicting the storming of a fortified city's walls. One attacker and one defender are armed with stirrup crossbows; on the extreme right, you can see a slinger from the feudal levy with wide-brimmed hat and small round shield. (Public domain, The Morgan Library and Museum)

Philip Augustus and he fought against England during the First Barons' War. By 1216, he had freed himself from any form of indirect English control and had transformed the Kingdom of Gwynedd into the dominant military power of Wales. In 1218, after his French allies had been expelled from England, the Welsh leader signed a treaty with Henry III. This confirmed him in possession of all his recent conquests, something that caused malcontent among the Marcher Lords (including William Marshal). In 1220, the sons of William Marshal and Llywelyn went to war against each other: the former attacked the territorial possessions of his enemy with an army coming from Ireland and could count on the support of the royal military forces. The conflict, which remained a local affair between the Marcher Lords and Llywelyn, ended in 1223 with the restoration of the status quo. In 1228, however, the Welsh warlord again attacked the English lands, and this time the royal army had to intervene on a large scale in order to support the Marcher Lords. Meanwhile, in 1219, William Marshal had died before completing the process of reforms that he had organised. Three men took the English government in their hands in place of the defunct regent: the Papal legate Pandulf Verraccio (died 16 September 1226), Peter des Roches (died 9 June 1238) and Hubert de Burgh. The ambitious Hubert removed Peter des Roches in 1221 by accusing him of treason; in that same year, Pandulf of Verraccio was recalled to Rome and thus Hubert remained as the only regent. Like his predecessor, Hubert de Burgh experienced

Mounted crossbowman equipped with nasal helmet. (Les Guerriers du Moyen-Age)

serious difficulties in dealing with Llywelyn in Wales; in addition, he had to face several minor revolts of some barons.

The weakness of Henry III was apparent, as he still did not have complete control over his own kingdom despite his regent's efforts. Hoping to take advantage of this situation, Louis VIII of France, who had been crowned king in 1187 after the death of his father Philip Augustus, decided to attack the English territorial possessions in Aquitaine (which were by now reduced to the regions of Poitou and Gascony). Poitou was easily conquered by the French, since the local nobles abandoned the young Henry III; part of Gascony was also occupied, but in 1225 an English army was sent to France with orders to reconquer it. In exchange for providing their support to the reconquest of Gascony, the English barons obtained from Henry III the promulgation of an enlarged and improved version of the Magna Carta. The young king assumed formal control of his government in January 1227; he richly rewarded Hubert de Burgh for his services and gave him many land possessions as a reward. In 1226, Louis VIII died, leaving the throne to his young son Louis IX (25 April 1214–25 August 1270), who was just 12 years old. The latter's rule was not accepted by some French nobles, and this caused the outbreak of several revolts in France; in 1228, some of the French aristocrats who were rebelling against Louis IX called upon Henry III to invade France. In particular Peter I (1187–26 May 1250), Duke of Brittany, openly revolted against the young Louis and gave his homage to the King of England. As a result, following these events, in 1230 Henry III decided to invade France. He set sail from Portsmouth at the head of a large force; the English troops landed at Saint-Malo in Brittany, where they joined forces with their French allies. Henry attacked the County of Anjou, but made little progress; he then went back to Brittany but finally decided to suspend his invasion of France having understood that the support of the French nobles for his cause was not a sincere one. Following the failure of Henry III's invasion of France, Hubert de Burgh fell from power; as a result, his old rival Peter des Roches returned to England and allied himself with the most important barons who were not happy with the king's rule. The monarch, in order to avoid the outbreak of a major rebellion, had no choice but to order the arrest of Hubert (who had been accused of robbery of royal funds by his rivals) and to give the responsibilities of government to Peter. The latter used his new personal power to damage all his personal enemies, like William Marshal's son, Richard (1191–1215 April 1234). As a result, a new civil war broke out between Peter des Roches and Richard Marshal, which saw several barons supporting the latter in defence of the rights contained in the Magna Carter. Richard was the most important of the Marcher Lords and thus could count on significant military forces; in addition, he had vast land possessions in Ireland and even formed an alliance with the Welsh Llywelyn. In 1234, the Archbishop of Canterbury intervened in order to stop the hostilities, which finally ended when Peter de Roches was removed from his institutional role and Richard Marshal died. The civil conflict had negative consequences for Henry III's position in France, since Brittany was reconquered by the French while he was fighting in his own kingdom. After the events of 1230–1234, the king decided to rule his realm in an autonomous way and left the important post of Justiciar vacant inside the royal government. The position of Chancellor was deprived of most of its original powers. All the most important decisions started to be taken directly by the king, who was influenced only by the advice of his closest friends. However, Henry III was not a tyrannical monarch and respected the Magna Carta on most occasions. He also held large gatherings of nobles at his royal court, which started to be commonly known as 'parliaments'. These usually took place periodically when the king wanted to raise some 'special taxes', one-off levies that were used to fund a particular royal project like a military expedition. With the progression of time, the barons participated in the parliaments alongside some representatives of the middle class, who were sent to the court to pursue the interests of their home counties. The network of royal sheriffs created by King John declined during Henry III's reign and local justice went back under

Peasant infantryman armed with staff sling. (Milites Pagenses)

the control of the local nobles. While popular with some, this greatly affected the collection of taxes, since it became difficult for the monarch to exploit the large debts owed to the Crown by the barons.

During 1242–1243, Henry III was involved in a new French conflict, known as 'Saintonge War' from the name of the region where it was fought. Having been lost by King John, the County of Poitou had become part of the French territorial domains; Louis VIII had given it to his second oldest son, Alphonse (11 November 1220–21 August 1271), while his first son became his successor on the French throne. The Poitevin barons were against the idea of having the King of France's brother as their feudal overlord and thus, when Alphonse came of age, they revolted against him. The rebellion was led by the most powerful of the Poitevin nobles, Hugh X of Lusignan (c.1183–c.5 June 1249). The barons of Poitou wanted to have Richard of Cornwall (5 January 1209–2 April 1272), the younger brother of Henry III, as their count and asked the English monarch to support them in their rebellion. Louis IX assembled a very large army to help his brother and marched against the castle of Montreuil-Bonnin, which was the main stronghold of the Lusignan family. Meanwhile, Henry III assembled a force of 30,000 soldiers and set sail from Portsmouth. The King of England wanted to reconquer Poitou and considered this as a first step towards the restoration of the empire that had been lost by his father. On 20 July 1242, the decisive battle between Henry III and Louis IX took place at Taillebourg, near the Charente River. Both sides had around 20,000 infantrymen each, but the French had 4,000 heavy knights and the English just 1,600. The English attacked first, but they were soon repulsed; the following counter-attack of the French knights was absolutely devastating and decided the outcome of the clash when the strategic bridge crossing the Charente River was occupied by Louis IX's men. After their victory, the French conquered the rebel city of Saintes and obliged Hugh of Lusignan to surrender. Fearing that Louis IX could now also invade his possessions in Aquitaine, Henry III organised a naval blockade of the French port city of La Rochelle in order to distract part of the French troops. This operation, however, failed and the king was forced to ask for a truce. Following defeat in the Saintonge War, Henry III had to abandon his plans for the reconquest of the Angevin lands in France. On 4 December 1259, he signed a lasting peace treaty with Louis IX in Paris, according to which the English monarch was given the territory of Guyenne in exchange for renouncing all his claims on French lands.

While these events took place on the continent, Henry III also had to deal with his rivals in the British Isles. In 1240, the Welsh warlord Llywelyn the Great died and this enabled the English to expand their presence in Wales. The king launched three minor military campaigns in the region during the 1240s, which resulted in the building of several new castles as well as the expansion of the County of Chester. However, in 1256, a major revolt broke out in Wales, but Henry III was unable to crush it due to the internal difficulties that he was experiencing in England; as a result, by the end of it, the general situation had gone back to the state of 1240. Ireland was mostly used by Henry III as a reserve of fiefdoms that could be given to his most loyal supporters as a reward for their services. The warlike English barons of Ireland continued to fight some local wars with the Irish princedoms and gradually expanded their own territorial domains, but the complete English conquest of the island was still unrealistic. Regarding Scotland, Henry III was able to maintain peace along the northern borders of his realm; Alexander II of Scotland married Henry's sister Joan (22 July 1210–4 March 1238) in 1221 and signed the important Treaty of York with the English monarch in 1237. In 1251, Alexander II's son and heir, the future Alexander III of Scotland (4 September 1241–19 March 1286), was knighted by Henry III and married his daughter Margaret (29 September 1240–26 February 1275). On the continent, the King of England had to defend his possessions in Gascony not only from the French but also from Alfonso X of Castile (23 November 1221–4 April 1284). Alfonso instigated a violent uprising of the Gascons in 1252, and Henry was forced to intervene personally and carry on an expensive military campaign to secure his control over Gascony. Eventually, an agreement was made through which Gascony was assigned to Henry III's son Edward (17/18 June 1239–7 July 1307), who married Alfonso X's half-sister Eleanor.

During the second half of his long reign, the King of England tried to obtain a realm for his younger son Edmund (16 January 1245–5 June 1296) and thus turned his attention towards the Kingdom of Sicily. The kingdom had been ruled by the Holy Roman Emperor Frederick II (26 December 1194–13 December 1250), enemy of the papacy, until 1250. When Frederick died, the throne of Sicily was taken by Manfred (1232–26 February 1266), a natural son of the deceased Emperor; Pope Innocent IV (c.1195–7 December 1254), however, considered Manfred to be an 'abusive monarch' and thus decided to start looking for a new ruler for southern Italy. In 1254, Henry and Innocent IV reached an agreement according to which Edmund would be the new King of Sicily after defeating Manfred and his supporters; soon after this, however, the Pope died and was replaced by Alexander IV. Alexander refused to fund the English war effort in the Kingdom of Sicily as agreed by his predecessor and offered the crown of southern Italy to Louis IX's younger brother, Charles (1227–85), who defeated Manfred in 1260 and conquered the contested realm.

From 1258, Henry III had to face a series of internal problems, which were mostly caused by the raising of large sums of money to fund the military campaigns and the diplomatic policies of the monarch. The royal government was always short of money, and this had some very negative consequences over its effective military capabilities. In April 1258, the discontent of the barons erupted when seven of them, including the powerful Simon de Montfort (c.1208–4 August 1265), formed an aristocratic alliance

Peasant infantryman armed with staff sling. (Les Guerriers du Moyen-Age)

Above left: Early form of nasal helmet. (Historia Aquitanorum).

Above right: Nasal helmet. (Les Seigneurs d'Orient)

with the objective of forcing the king to create a council – exclusively made up of prominent pro-Simon nobles and clergymen – to help him in taking the most important decisions and in governing the country. The king, hoping to avoid a full-scale civil war, agreed; the pressure for political reforms, however, continued during the following months. The monarch had to accept the creation of a second and smaller council made up of 15 members, all elected by the barons, which had the power to appoint the most important members of the English royal government (Justiciar, Chancellor and Treasurer). At this point, two opposing factions started to emerge among the English barons: one, led by Simon de Montfort, asked for radical reforms that would have limited the authority and power of the Crown as well as the major nobles; the other, guided by Hugh Bigod (c.1182–18 February 1225), promoted only moderate changes and was more favourable to Henry III. Edward, the king's son and heir, allied himself with Simon de Montfort and helped him to pass the radical 'Provisions of Westminster' in 1259, which introduced great limits on the royal officials. In 1260, tension continued to grow between the Crown and the barons, despite Edward's reconciliation with his father. By the summer of 1261, the English nobles, guided by Simon de Montfort and by the king's younger brother Richard, had organised an autonomous 'parliament' and were already preparing for war. Henry III responded by raising a good number of foreign mercenaries and was temporarily able to gain the upper hand; he attempted to settle the political crisis of his realm by forcing the barons to agree a new treaty, which introduced a system of arbitration to settle the most important disputes existing between the Crown and the aristocrats. This attempt, however, failed, because the monarch soon started to target those barons who had revolted against him and to damage them both personally and professionally. After the death of the king's younger brother Richard and the Pope's decision to consider the 'Provisions of Westminster' as legitimate, open civil war finally broke out and the conflict commonly known as the 'Second Barons' War' began.

In April 1263, Simon de Montfort gathered a council of dissident barons in Oxford, while fighting broke out in the Welsh Marches. The rebel nobles were able to assemble a substantial army and marched on London; here, the population revolted against the king and trapped him in the Tower of London. After he arrived in the capital, Simon assumed effective control of England; the general support that he had in these early weeks of the war, however, soon disappeared since some barons – who opposed his personal supremacy – liberated Henry III. At this point, the king tried to mediate with the rebels and appealed to Louis IX for arbitration. In January 1264, the King of France declared his support for Henry, but his decision was not accepted by Simon de Montfort and by the most radical barons. Effective fighting resumed in February, when the rebels attacked the royalist supporters of the Welsh Marches and defeated them. The hostilities continued with the siege of Northampton by the royalists, where the rebel barons tried to free the besieged city but failed to do so. After this, Simon went with most of his troops to Kent, where he started besieging the important castle of Rochester. The siege, however, had to be abandoned very soon since the royalist forces started to advance on London. Unexpectedly, Henry III decided to not invest his capital but to move to Rochester in order to relieve the local garrison; he then captured the towns of Tonbridge and Winchelsea from the rebels. Henry III then moved into Sussex, where he was confronted by Simon de Montfort and the Battle of Lewes took place (14 May 1264). The king had a clear numerical advantage, since he commanded 10,000 men; the barons, in comparison, had just 5,000 knights and soldiers. The clash began with a very effective royalist charge led by Henry's son Edward, which crushed one wing of the baronial army; the young prince, however, followed the defeated enemies in close pursuit and left his father alone on the main battlefield. Having no choice, Henry III ordered a general assault in the hope of breaking the enemy's strong defensive positions, which were located on higher ground. The attack was repulsed by the reserves of Simon de Montfort and the royalists lost the battle; trying to avoid further human losses, Henry III left the battlefield. After the defeat of Lewes, the monarch had to send Edward to Simon de Montfort as a hostage and was obliged to sign a document that recognised the new 'Provisions of Oxford' (written by the rebels) as a legitimate document. In May 1265, however, Edward escaped from baronial custody and was able to assemble a new royalist army. At this point of the war, several nobles abandoned Simon de Montfort and joined Edward, since they considered the reforms projected by their former leader as potentially dangerous for the survival of the aristocracy. After these defections, Simon could not avoid the royalist conquest of Gloucester and decided to move into Wales in order to forge an alliance with the local warlords, who provided him with some military contingents. Edward proved to be an excellent military commander during this phase of the conflict: he attacked the main stronghold of Simon, the castle of Kenilworth, and besieged it with great determination. The barons responded to this by crossing the Severn River and trying to reach Kenilworth in order to remove the siege. The royalist army, however, moved to intercept Simon de Montfort, and the decisive Battle of Evesham was fought on 4 August 1265. Once again, the royalists had a clear numerical advantage, since Edward had 10,000 men and Simon de Montfort just 5,000.

In this battle, the young prince had learned from past experience and thus occupied the higher ground of the battlefield before the arrival of his enemies. The barons attacked first and invested the centre of the royalist army; after some initial success, however, their Welsh contingents abandoned the fighting. Edward rapidly surrounded the numerically inferior enemies and a terrible cavalry clash began. This soon became a real massacre for the barons, many of whom were killed, and Simon de Montfort and one of his sons died on the battlefield. The usual practice of capturing enemy nobles in order to obtain a ransom was temporarily forgotten at Evesham in favour of execution. Victory had been complete for Edward, who was now ready to rule his realm as a king in place of his old father (who played no significant role in the final part of the conflict). The war lasted for some months, since the rebels continued to defend their strongholds with desperate determination. In order to avoid further bloodshed, Henry III drafted a proclamation known as the 'Dictum of Kenilworth' according to which all rebels could obtain royal pardon and regain their confiscated lands on payment of a fine. On 14 December, the last defenders of the castle of Kenilworth surrendered and accepted the terms of the dictum. The last groups of rebels continued to fight until the summer of 1267, when they downed arms at the Isle of Ely (their last stronghold). Some months after these events, in November, the 'Statute of Marlborough' replaced the Provisions of Oxford with the previous and more moderate Provisions of Westminster. In that same autumn, Henry III also made peace with the Welsh princes who had supported the rebel barons. The last years of Henry's long reign saw him increasingly infirm and thus his son Edward started to play a prominent role in the government of the realm. The monarch died on 16 November 1272, at Westminster, while his son Edward was fighting against Islamic warriors in the Eighth Crusade. The new king came back to England only some months later.

Left: Detail of the hood of chainmail that was worn under the helmet. (Historia Aquitanorum)

Below: Miniature from the folio 34 recto of the Morgan Bible, representing an army marching out from the walls of a fortified city. The professional foot soldiers following the knights are equipped like the latter and are armed with battle staffs or poleaxes. (Public domain, The Morgan Library and Museum)

Above: Miniature from the folio 43 verso of the Morgan Bible, representing an army besieging a walled city. On the left, it is possible to see a traction trebuchet manned by feudal levies, one of the most effective siege weapons of the Middle Ages. (Public domain, The Morgan Library and Museum)

Right: Nice example of a 'mask' helmet. (Les Guerriers du Moyen-Age)

Chapter 9

The Reign of Edward I
1272–1307

After being crowned King of England, Edward I soon turned his attention to the frontiers of his realm with one ambitious objective in mind: making England the dominant power of the British Isles by conquering the territories of Wales, Scotland and Ireland. The first target of the new expansionist policy of England were the princedoms of Wales, which had been at war several times with the Crown since the days of William the Conqueror. As previously discussed, the Marcher Lords had gradually been able to conquer a good portion of southern Wales, while the northern region of the country was still dominated by some independent local kingdoms. The most important of these was that of Gwynedd, which was the leading military power of Wales since it had transformed the smaller princedoms of Powys and Deheubarth into tributary states. The princes of Gwynedd assumed the honorific title of 'Prince of Wales' when ascending to their throne and their authority had been recognised by the English kings. By the time of Edward I's coronation, Gwynedd was ruled by Llywelynn ap Gruffudd (c.1223–11 December 1282), who was a strong and experienced military leader like his predecessor, Llywelynn the Great. In 1267, the Welsh princes had signed a peace treaty with Henry III, but very soon after they had resumed hostilities against the Marcher Lords. The latter were unhappy with the Crown's policy for Wales, since they were convinced that the right moment had come to conquer Wales. For decades, the English had fought wars of expansion on the continent, in the hope of consolidating the Angevin territorial possessions in France; now that the monarchs of France were too strong to be defeated, English expansionism had to find new objectives. Wales and Ireland were an obvious choice, since they had already been partly occupied during the previous centuries. In 1274, Edward just needed a 'casus belli' to attack Gwynedd and he soon found it: two Welsh nobles attempted to assassinate Llywelynn but their plans failed and then they defected to the English. One of them was Llywelynn's younger brother. Due to these events, the Welsh prince refused to give his formal homage to the King of England, as the latter was supporting his internal enemies. In November 1276, war was declared.

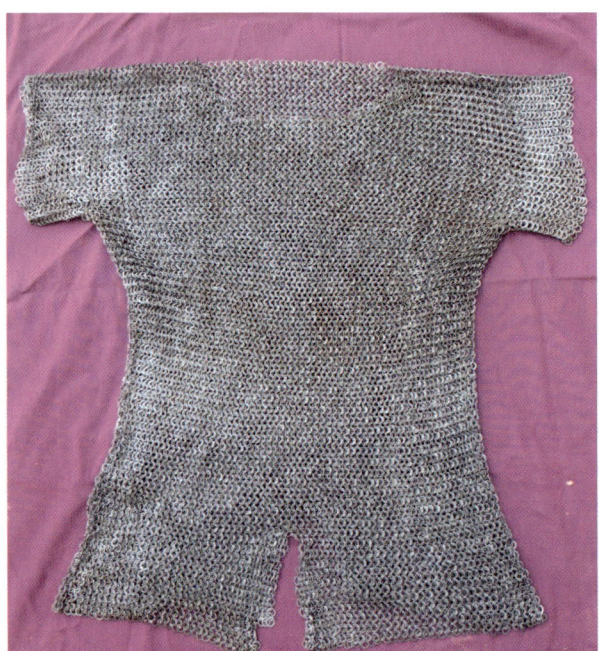

Short-sleeved hauberk of chainmail. (Les Seigneurs d'Orient)

In July 1277, Edward I launched his first invasion of Wales, at the head of an army comprising 15,000 men; 9,000 of these were Welshmen who were against Llywelynn's rule or who came from minor princedoms. The campaign saw no pitched battles, since the Welsh were not used to fighting on the open field against large English armies comprising a good number of heavy knights. Cavalry was a very minor component of the Welsh armies, which were mostly made up of light infantry skirmishers and archers. On the open field, the Welsh light infantry had no chance of defeating the English heavy cavalry; the sturdy Welsh fighters, however, were very effective in launching hit-and-run attacks as well as in using 'guerrilla' methods. They had a perfect knowledge of their home territories, the nature of which was still very wild, and could easily organise deadly ambushes and incursions against the foreign invaders. However, Llywelynn could not count on large popular support and therefore had no choice but to surrender without having fought a single proper battle. According to the Treaty of Aberconwy, which was signed in November 1277, Gwynedd could no longer exert any form of political influence over the other Welsh princedoms but remained independent. War broke out again in 1282, but this time it was fought with a higher level of intensity. Edward had launched merely a punitive expedition in 1277; now he wanted to occupy Wales in a stable way. The Welsh knew this, and thus united all their forces to resist the invasion. The first phase of the conflict was particularly favourable to the Welsh, who obtained a couple of minor victories and organised a series of effective ambushes against the English. On 11 December 1282, however, Llywelynn and his army of 7,000 warriors were defeated in a decisive way at the Battle of Orewin Bridge: the arrows of the English archers and a charge of the English heavy knights killed hundreds of Welsh fighters, including Llywelynn, who had made a fatal mistake, since he had decided to face the English on the open field. Following this clash, which proved decisive for the history of the British Isles, Gwynedd was rapidly occupied by Edward I.

In 1284, with the Statute of Rhuddlan, the Principality of Wales was incorporated into the Kingdom of England and given a new administrative system with counties policed by sheriffs. In order to secure his possession over the newly conquered territories, Edward I initiated a full-scale 'colonisation' of Wales by building new towns as well as new castles in several areas of the country. Many English migrants were encouraged to move to Wales, in order to populate the new settlements. The network of castles created by the English was particularly strong and was designed to prevent any future uprising. The title of 'Prince of Wales' would now be given to the heir to the English throne, starting from Edward I's son Edward ([25 April 1284–21 September 1327] the future Edward II). From an administrative point of view, the territory of Wales was partitioned between the Crown and the English barons who had supported the conquest of the country (most notably the Marcher Lords). Those local rulers of central

Detail of the iron rings making up a chainmail. (Historia Aquitanorum)

Detail of a mitten made of chainmail. (Sericum et ferrum)

Wales who had fought on Edward's side during the war retained their territorial possessions, but they were no longer princes since they were, instead, being transformed into normal fiefs of the English Crown. In just a few years, the Welsh lands underwent a radical process of change: feudalism was introduced, together with English common law; and Welsh law continued to be used only for some civil cases and gradually disappeared. Edward's reign saw several Welsh rebellions, most notably in 1287 and 1294: these, however, were all crushed by the English authorities, mostly thanks to the presence of their strong castles made of stone, which were impossible for the Welsh insurgents to conquer. By conquering Wales, Edward I had eliminated one of the main elements menacing the stability of his realm's borders; in addition, he had obtained the unconditioned loyalty of the powerful Marcher Lords.

Edward was an excellent monarch in many ways; he restored order in his kingdom after the disastrous experiences of the Second Barons' War and re-established royal authority over the nobility. He fought against all the abuses of power committed by the royal officials in the various territories and of the aristocrats with the same energy. The king made a full revision of all the rights enjoyed by the barons, in order to understand if some of them were 'abusive' towards the Crown; in addition, he started to involve some new social groups in the administration of the realm. During his reign, the role played by merchants became increasingly important; in exchange for this, however, they had to pay customs duties to the Crown and their money was used by Edward to fund his military campaigns. In 1295, continuing his process of reforms, the king opened up parliament meetings to knights and representatives of the boroughs, and the commons started to be involved in the making of major political decisions.

After completing the conquest of Wales, Edward turned his attention to Scotland. Broadly speaking, the Anglo-Scottish relations of the previous decades had been quite positive since the Scottish monarchs had renounced their expansionist ambitions over Northern England. During the years 1281–1284, however, the three children of Alexander III of Scotland died one after the other, and, in 1286, Alexander himself died. Consequently, the Scottish crown was given to the defunct king's granddaughter, Margaret (1283–September 1290), who was just three years old at the time. The international position of Scotland was severely damaged by these unexpected and tragic events, and Edward I took them as an opportunity to exert his influence over the Scottish monarchy. In 1286, the Treaty of Birgham was signed between England and Scotland: according to this, it was agreed that Margaret would marry Edward I's son, Edward, but that the Kingdom of Scotland would remain free from English overlordship. In the autumn of 1290, however, the heir to the Scottish throne fell ill and died: as a result, Scotland remained without an obvious heir and a very complex succession crisis began (which is commonly known as the 'Great Cause'). As many as 14 different 'potential' heirs put forward their claims to the title of King of Scotland, but very soon it became apparent that the dynastic battle for the destiny of Scotland would be fought between two

Miniature from the folio 3 verso of the Morgan Bible, showing a surprise attack launched against a military encampment. The infantrymen on the right have been surprised by their enemies and are still trying to put on their padded aketons or chainmail hauberks; the attackers on the left, two of whom have padded infulae for protection of the head, are armed with axe and fauchard. The latter was a deadly infantry weapon consisting of a scythe-like blade, with a point at the top and a hook at the back (specifically designed to unhorse knights). (Public domain, The Morgan Library and Museum)

pretenders: John Balliol (c.1249–late 1314) and Robert the Bruce (11 July 1274–7 June 1329). Since the realm was on the verge of civil war, the Scottish aristocrats asked Edward I to conduct the proceedings of the succession process; they, however, did not ask the English monarch to be the sole arbitrator in the ongoing dispute.

The final decision was to be made by 104 auditors: 40 appointed by Balliol, 40 appointed by Bruce and 24 selected by Edward I from senior members of the Scottish nobility. Edward was determined to become the overlord of Scotland and thus decided to help the Scottish aristocrats only to pursue his own political interests. He insisted that, if he was to help settle the ongoing dynastic contest, he had to be recognised as the Kingdom of Scotland's feudal overlord. The Scottish nobles were initially reluctant to make such an important concession to the foreign king, but eventually they agreed that the realm would have been handed over to Edward until a rightful heir was found. After long discussions, which were partly influenced by the English monarch, the auditors made their decision in favour of John Balliol on 17 November 1292. After the new Scottish king was chosen, however, Edward I refused to give up his control over Scotland; Balliol soon became a 'puppet' in his hands, while Scottish administration started to be managed by the English Crown. This new situation was unacceptable for the Scottish nobles, who were now required to provide military forces to Edward for his military campaigns. As a result, a major rebellion broke out in Scotland with an attack on Carlisle; the King of England responded by launching a massive invasion of the country in 1296. After sacking Berwick-upon-Tweed, he besieged the important castle of Dunbar; the Scots responded by sending a relief force to the besieged stronghold, but this was

Detail showing how the spurs were worn over chainmail. (Les Guerriers du Moyen-Age)

routed by the English heavy cavalry at the Battle of Dunbar (27 April 1296). This was not a large clash – since it consisted of a fight between two small groups of heavy knights – but caused the surrender of Dunbar's garrison. In addition, it showed the great tactical superiority that the English heavy cavalrymen had over their Scottish equivalents. After these defeats, Edward I advanced unopposed into the heart of the Scottish territory and deposed Balliol, who was then imprisoned in the Tower of London. English officials took over the Scottish government and Edward came back to England. The destiny of Scotland, however, had not yet been definitively decided.

The military campaigns of Edward I put a great financial demand on his subjects, especially due to the introduction of an unpopular additional duty on wool that was very damaging to merchants. The fiscal demands of the Crown also caused resentment among the nobles and the clergymen. In 1294, the king made a demand for a grant of one half of all clerical revenues in order to fund his planned military expeditions in France and Ireland; this was agreed, despite some opposition, and was followed by a second demand after a few months. In 1296, however, the attitude of the English clergy changed radically when the papal bull 'Clericis laicos' was promulgated: this bull prohibited the clergy to pay taxes to any authority without receiving explicit consent from the Pope. Fearing the negative consequences, the Archbishop of Canterbury did nothing to apply the papal bull in England and thus the resistance of the clergy to Edward's taxation did not last for long. Despite the internal opposition from the clergymen and nobles, the King of England was finally able to fund a 'continental expedition' in 1297. Three years before, the Count of Flanders, Guy (c.1226–7 March 1305), had tried to conclude an alliance with Edward I by arranging a marriage between his daughter Philippa (died 1306) and the Prince of Wales, Edward II. This, however, was perceived as a threat to the stability of his realm by the new King of France, Philip IV (1268–29 November 1314), who imprisoned Guy and forced him to call off the planned marriage.

The County of Flanders had a very special political status at the time: being on the frontier of two states, its rulers gave homage to both the King of France and the Holy Roman Emperor. Furthermore, English merchants had very strong commercial interests in Flanders. In 1296, the most important cities of the region were taken under French protection; at this point, Guy asked for Edward I's help, but in 1297 a large French army invaded the County of Flanders with orders to annex it into Philip IV's domains. Initially, the English tried to support their Flemish allies by attacking the French from Aquitaine, but their initiatives failed; as a result, in August 1297, Edward I landed with 900 knights and 7,500 infantrymen on the Flemish coast. After some weeks of fighting that saw no major engagements, the mediation of the Pope led to the signing of an armistice in October. Edward left the continent without having achieved any significant result; this was mostly due to the fact that a large uprising had just begun in Scotland and the King of England was needed to deal with it.

During the previous months, discontent had been growing in Scotland since the new English administrators were particularly hated by the local population. Two new leaders emerged in the country, who were to play an important role in the upcoming revolt: Andrew de Moray (died 1297) and William Wallace (c.1270–23 August 1305). The first was the son of an important noble and had been captured by the English during the Battle of Dunbar; after escaping, he gathered a group of insurgents who started to attack the English by using hit-and-run tactics. The activities of these insurgents were particularly successful and freed the entire province of Moray from Edward I's men. William Wallace was a minor noble who rose to prominence in May 1297, when he killed the English sheriff of Lanark and started his own rebellion against the foreign invaders. When news of the revolt initiated by William rippled throughout Scotland, thousands of free men – most notably Highlanders – rallied to him and enlarged the insurgent forces at his command. Very soon, Wallace started to be supported by the Bishop of Glasgow and by Sir William Douglas, who was a respected noble; as a result, what had begun as a popular but local revolt transformed itself into a national rebellion. William obtained a series of victories and occupied Scone, the seat of the English-appointed Justiciar of Scotland; as a result, Edward I decided to intervene in order to restore his control over the northern part of Scotland. He ordered Robert the Bruce to attack William Douglas' possessions in Lanarkshire, but while on the march the pretender to the Scottish throne

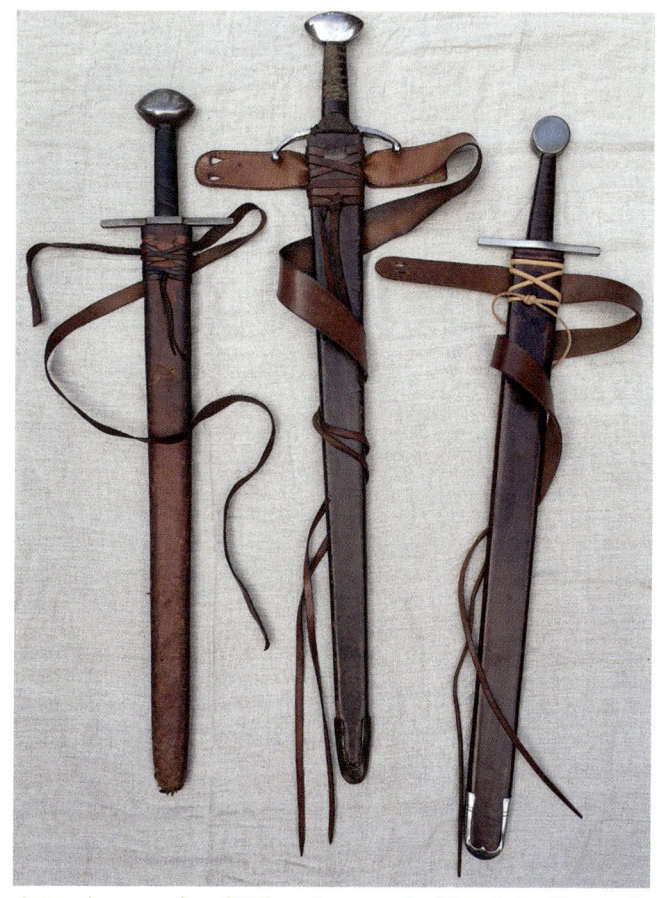

Some nice examples of 13th century swords. (Historia Aquitanorum).

Some nice examples of 13th century swords. (Milites Pagenses)

decided to join the rebellion and disobeyed the King of England. At this point, the revolt was already becoming a full-scale war, since Robert the Bruce's example was followed by most of the Scottish nobles. Meanwhile, Moray and Wallace continued to raise and train an increasing number of free men; they attacked the English on several occasions and in a relatively short time they forced them south of the Forth River, leaving Edward's forces in possession only of the castle of Dundee. William Wallace initiated the siege of the fortification but was soon informed that an English army under the Earl of Surrey was marching against him. At this point, the Scottish leader, who had united his forces with those of Moray, decided to face the English on the open field in order to defend the bridge that crossed the Forth River at Stirling.

On 11 September 1297, the iconic Battle of Stirling Bridge took place. From a military point of view, Wallace's decision to fight a pitched clash against the English was extremely audacious: his forces consisted of just 6,000 infantrymen and 300 knights, while John de Warenne (1231–27 September 1304), the Earl of Surrey had 7,000 infantrymen and 2,000 heavy cavalrymen. Until that moment, at least in the British Isles, an infantry force had never been able to defeat a strong contingent of feudal knights on the open field; the Scottish foot soldiers were not trained to fight in close formation and had little chance of stopping a cavalry charge conducted by knights equipped with chainmail. The Scottish forces, however, had a great tactical advantage at Stirling since the English knights had to cross the narrow bridge in order to attack their defensive positions. Wallace and Moray made the English cross the bridge unmolested during the first phase of the battle; however, when the number of English soldiers who had crossed the river reached 2,000, they launched a furious attack. The English knights who had completed the crossing charged against the Scottish infantrymen, but they were too few and were repulsed. At this point, the Scottish soldiers gained control of the east side of the bridge and encircled those English soldiers who had crossed the river. What followed was a real massacre, since the 2,000 English knights and infantrymen who had been trapped were all killed. Despite this, the bulk of the Earl of Surrey's army remained intact; the English commander could have launched a new attack, but his initial confidence was gone: he ordered the bridge to be destroyed and retreated towards Berwick. The Lowlands of Scotland had been abandoned to the rebels, who had obtained a first important victory over the English. The Battle of Stirling Bridge was particularly important especially from a psychological point of view, since it showed that the English heavy knights could be defeated by the Scottish infantrymen. During the clash, however, Andrew Moray was severely wounded and died a few days later. Over the following weeks, William Wallace expelled the last English military contingents from Scotland and organised an invasion of Northern England. He entered Northumberland and pillaged the latter region, without meeting opposition.

In March 1298, after returning to Scotland, William was appointed 'Guardian of the Kingdom' in the name of the exiled king John Balliol. Meanwhile, Edward I was reorganising his military forces for a new attack against Scotland and had established his main base at York. The English invasion began in July and culminated with the famous Battle of Falkirk (22 July 1298). The English army assembled by Edward comprised the following elements: 2,000 heavy cavalrymen, 10,000 Welsh infantrymen, 2,000 archers and 500 mercenary crossbowmen. William Wallace commanded 4,000 infantrymen, supported by 1,000 cavalrymen and 1,000 archers. The 4,000 Scottish foot soldiers were all equipped as spearmen and were organised into four 'hedgehogs' known as 'schiltrons'. These were compact close formations, very similar to the infantry phalanxes of Antiquity; since their members were armed with long pikes, they were specifically designed to resist cavalry charges. During the previous months, William Wallace had improved the training of his infantrymen a lot, transforming them into an elite combat force; the English knights had never faced an infantry contingent with the same quality of schiltrons and had no idea of their opponents' tactics. Wallace filled the gaps between his four infantry formations with archers and deployed his small cavalry on the back of the schiltrons as a reserve. He occupied a strong defensive position and had no intention of abandoning it. Edward ordered a general charge of his cavalry, which was organised into four 'battles' or brigades which advanced in echelon formation. For the first time in the military history of the British Isles, a massive charge of the feudal cavalry was blocked and defeated by the infantry: the spearmen of the schiltrons repulsed the enemy assaults with their 'forest of pikes' and killed a large number of English knights. After the defeat of his best troops, Edward I did not abandon the battlefield but instead decided to attack the schiltrons with his excellent longbowmen: they fired thousands of arrows against the static infantry formations of the Scots, who were a very easy target. The mercenary crossbowmen attacked the enemy infantry with their deadly darts. The Scottish infantrymen suffered extremely severe losses during this phase of the clash and their formations lost cohesion; when the Welsh infantrymen and the English cavalrymen launched a second attack, the schiltrons were broken up and the surviving Scottish infantrymen had to abandon the field. Edward I had won the Battle of Falkirk thanks to his archers, but his cavalry had suffered serious losses and had been humiliated by a contingent of 'plebeian' infantry. As a result, after the clash, he decided to leave Scotland and went back to York.

In May 1300, the King of England organised a new campaign against Scotland, but this only saw some skirmishing and ended with a truce that was sponsored by Pope Boniface VIII (c.1230–11 October 1303). Meanwhile, the Scottish nobles had started to fight against each other in order to determine the identity of their next king. Hoping to gain advantage from this situation, in 1301 the English organised a new invasion of Scotland and assembled two armies. This time, however, Edward made very little progress against the Scots and thus was forced to stop the military operations after accepting another truce. In November 1302, the hostilities resumed and saw some minor victories for the Scots; meanwhile, however, Robert the Bruce had decided – temporarily – to support Edward I in the hope of being chosen

Above: Miniature from the folio 24 verso of the Morgan Bible, representing the looting operations that usually followed the success of a 'chevauchée' (raid). On the right, you can see some captured infantrymen being carried away together with some stolen cattle (which were fundamental for feeding the feudal armies while on campaign). (Public domain, The Morgan Library and Museum)

Left: Quiver of a longbow. (Milites Pagenses)

by the English monarch as the next King of Scotland. In May 1303, another English invasion of Scotland took place. King Edward occupied Edinburgh and reconquered most of Scotland without facing a serious opposition, due to the internal divisions experienced by his enemies. After campaigning in the Highlands, the English were finally able to force the Scots into surrender. The terms of submission stipulated in February 1303, however, were not accepted by William Wallace, who continued to fight with his followers. In the following months, Edward I took all the necessary steps for a final annexation of Scotland to the Kingdom of England, and, on 3 August 1305, Wallace was finally captured and sent to London where he was executed as a traitor. The hopes of the Scots now rested on Robert the Bruce, who had allied himself with the English only to gain enough time to secure his position as next King of Scotland. Having eliminated his Scottish rivals and obtaining support from most of the Scottish nobles, Robert finally rebelled against Edward I and was crowned King of Scotland on 25 March 1306.

Robert assembled a new army and launched a new military campaign to free his realm from the English presence. At the Battle of Methven, on 19 June 1306, the Scottish troops were easily crushed by the English and Robert ran the risk of being captured. Following this defeat, he had to abandon mainland Scotland and could do nothing to save his family from Edward I's cruel revenge: most of his relatives were captured by the English and his three brothers were executed. In February 1307, however, Robert resumed his efforts to liberate Scotland from the foreign invaders and started re-gathering men. Some months later, at the Battle of Loudoun Hill (10 May 1307), he obtained a minor victory over the English and his number of followers continued to grow. On 6 July 1307, before he could organise a new campaign against Robert the Bruce, Edward I of England died in his camp located just south of the Scottish border having developed dysentery. His heir and successor, Edward II, abandoned Northern England, where he was preparing for battle, in late August, and was crowned king on 25 February 1308.

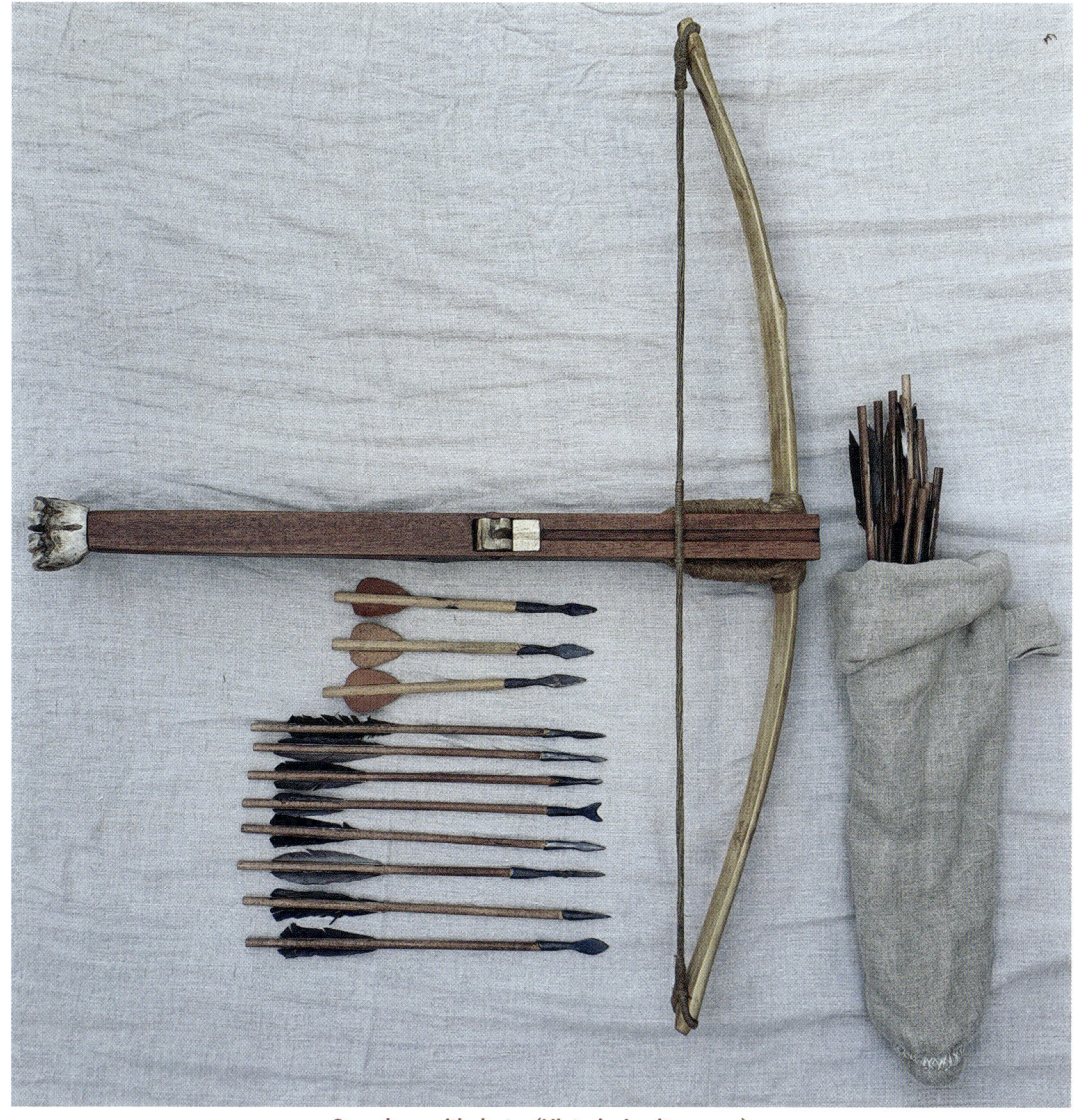

Crossbow with darts. (Historia Aquitanorum).

Chapter 10
Military Organisation and Equipment in the Medieval British Isles

England

With the Norman conquest of 1066, feudalism was brought to the Kingdom of England from the Duchy of Normandy, when William the Conqueror parcelled the lands of his new realm out to the barons who had fought at his orders at the Battle of Hastings. According to the latest calculations, around 5,000 knights were enfeoffed (i.e., given a fiefdom) by King William during the first phase of his reign. The English lands were not given only to lay barons, but also to clerical nobles who were 'Princes of the Church'. Each baron, lay or clerical, was required to provide the knights who were at his orders to the king in case of war. According to the Cartae Baronum of 1166, a compilation of data detailing the military obligations of all the English nobles, 784 knights out of 5,000 were to be provided by clerical barons. With the progression of time, the military system based on sub-infeudation – i.e., the division of the barons' major fiefdoms into minor ones given to knights – became increasingly complex. An important military document dated 1181 – the so-called 'Assize of Arms' – prescribed that, when the number of knights sub-infeudated within his fiefdom fell short of the knight-service owed to the monarch, a single feudal tenant should maintain sufficient equipment to supply the knights in his personal household in order to make up the difference. Most of the English nobles had personal households consisting of loyal knights who provided military service in exchange for money and not for land. These retinues of professional soldiers could consist of just a few individuals but also of larger contingents, depending on the wealth of the baron paying them. The compulsory military service based on the feudal military structure – known as 'servitium debitum' – could last for a maximum of 60 days (later reduced to 40) after mobilisation. Initially, the mobilised feudal knights could also be sent to fight overseas, to protect the Norman (and later Plantagenet) territorial possessions in France, but following John Lackland's reign most of the English milites refused to serve outside the British Isles.

Some major nobles were granted what was known as 'money fief', i.e. they were not required to send their knights to the king in case of war but had to provide a fixed sum of money with which the monarch could recruit mercenary soldiers. This system, however, never became particularly popular in the Plantagenet domains. Feudal military mobilisations usually caused malcontent among the barons of the realm, who were interested in pursuing their own personal interests more than those of the monarchy. As a result, following 1157, the Plantagenet kings attempted to introduce a new form of 'partial mobilisation' that was based on a quota system. According to this, the monarch was to summon only a portion – one third – of those knights owing feudal military service and call upon those remaining at home to support the mobilised milites from an economic point of view through the scutage system. Scutage was based on a simple principle: if exempted from his military duties, each vassal was to pay a certain sum of money that was to be employed for buying/maintaining the

Miniature from the folio 39 recto of the Morgan Bible, depicting a clash of knights. Several of the helmets are painted with bright colours and the caparisons of the horses – like the surcoats of the milites – are in a single plain colour. (Public domain, The Morgan Library and Museum)

personal military equipment of those vassals who had been mobilised. By the end of John Lackland's reign, however, this system of partial mobilisation was no longer in use since it had failed to reach its objectives. The knights holding a fiefdom, however, were not the only professional soldiers who could be called to serve by a Plantagenet king. There were, in fact, also tenants of an inferior social status who were known as 'sergeants' who, despite not being nobles, had been given a land property by the monarchy in exchange for their military services. Originally, the sergeants were required to serve as heavy infantrymen, since they did not have the economic resources to maintain a horse; with the progression of time, however, many of them became rich enough to equip themselves exactly like the noble milites. It should be noted, however, that the number of sergeants living in the Kingdom of England always remained quite small – especially if compared with that of their equivalents serving under the King of France.

The personal household of the monarch, known as familia regis, consisted of a few hundred knights acting as the personal bodyguard of the king; these knights served for money and responded only to the monarch. The members of the royal household were usually organised into 'constabularies' that had an average strength of 100 milites stipendiarii or 'paid knights' each. The feudal knights, in comparison, served in small groups of 20–25 milites each that were known as 'conrois' and had their own distinctive banners. A variable number of conrois could be assembled together to form the larger 'batailles' or 'battles', the cavalry divisions deployed for pitched battles. Each knight, feudal or mercenary, was usually accompanied on the battlefield by one or two esquires; these played only an auxiliary role and were tasked with managing the three horses owned by each milite – the 'destrier' or 'war horse', the 'courser' employed for travelling long distances, and the 'rouncey' employed for transporting equipment – but could also fight as light cavalrymen in case of emergency. With the progression of time the royal household, in

Above: Miniature from the folio 41 recto of the Morgan Bible, showing a battle of knights. All the figures have no heraldic elements reproduced on their surcoats and are wearing chainmail hauberks. Most of the knights have great helms, while some have simpler conical helmets with or without nasal. The triangular shield of the king on the right has metal reinforcements on its external surface. Offensive weapons include spears, swords, axes and maces. (Public domain, The Morgan Library and Museum)

Left: Welsh warrior wearing padded jacket and leather cap. (Photo by Thomas Ortner and copyright to Armin Kaar)

addition to the milites stipendiarii, started to include increasing numbers of foreign mercenaries recruited from abroad (mostly from northern France).

Cavalry was not the only component of the Norman armies, which also included sizeable contingents of infantrymen. After the Norman conquest of England, the old 'fyrd' military system created by the Saxons a few centuries before was maintained. According to this system, each able-bodied free man aged 16-60 and living in any shire of the Kingdom of England could be called to serve by his overlord in case of war. Those individuals who refused military service were subject to fines or to the loss of their properties. A commoner, for example, was to pay a fine of 30 shillings if he neglected compulsory military service. Service in the fyrd was usually of a short duration and had practically no costs for the royal authorities, since the members of this 'general levy' were expected to provide their own arms/provisions and were not paid by the monarch for their military services. Originally, the fyrd was mobilised and organised on a local basis, according to the tribal subdivisions of the various communities; with the arrival of feudalism, it started to be managed by the feudal lords. Each knight could mobilise a certain number of peasants who lived and worked on his landed properties in order to form a small retinue of poorly equipped infantrymen. In case of large-scale foreign invasions, it was the king's responsibility to call up the 'national fyrd' that was made up of all the able-bodied men of his realm. Conditions of service for the national fyrd (also known as the 'great fyrd') and for the more common 'shire fyrd' were quite different, since in most cases the English commoners were not particularly happy about the idea of serving far from their homes for long periods of time. Most of the English freemen were peasants, who spent their lives working in the fields and following the natural cycles. As a result, on most occasions, service in the 'great fyrd' could last only for very limited periods of time – 60 days, later reduced to 40 – and the king had to pay his freemen if any additional period of service was needed. The three most important military documents of the early Plantagenet period – the 1181 'Assize of Arms', the 1242 'Assize' and the 1285 'Statute of Winchester' – all confirmed the existence of the feudal infantry levy. During the late Saxon period, a quota system of mobilisation existed inside the fyrd; on most occasions, only one freeman from each five hides of land was required to join the national fyrd when it was mobilised for a campaign. The selected individual was expected to be equipped with spear and shield; in addition, he was expected to have provisions for two months and to receive a wage of 4 shillings, both of which were provided by the other men living on the five hides of land from which he was levied. The Norman kings abolished payments for the members of the fyrd, since feudal military service was considered to be a duty for each peasant; during the last decades of the 12th century, however, the Plantagenets re-introduced them for when the peasant infantrymen were not serving abroad. During the late Saxon period, a new social class of lesser noblemen, the thegns, had emerged from the rural communities and had started to hold estates, the average size of which was five hides. These minor landowners, after the Norman conquest, were mostly transformed into sergeants and were frequently employed by knights as the commanders of their feudal infantry retinues. It should be noted, however, that the smallest contingents of peasant foot soldiers could be commanded by parish priests, while the largest ones were usually commanded by the local sheriffs. Sheriffs, introduced in England by the Normans, were royal officials responsible for keeping peace in the various shires and for arranging the annual shire payment owed to the king. During the Plantagenet period, the Kingdom of England did not have large urban centres and did not see the development of significant urban militias, which is very different from what happened in the Kingdom of France. Only London could mobilise a certain number of well-equipped infantrymen (around 6,000) who – in contrast to their equivalents of the feudal levy – were mostly craftsmen and merchants.

The Assize of Arms of 1181, a document promulgated by Henry II and detailing the kind of personal equipment that every knight and feudal infantryman had to carry in war, divided the commoners into three military categories according to their economic capabilities: those possessing at least 16 marks of chattels or rents – like the richest sergeants – were to equip themselves as knights with full panoply; those possessing at least 10 marks of chattels or rents – like the poorest sergeants – were to equip themselves as heavy infantrymen with helmet, hauberk of chainmail and spear; those possessing less than 10 marks of chattels or rents were to equip themselves with helmet, quilted aketon and spear. Shields, being defensive weapons, were not mentioned in the document but were carried by all soldiers. Quite curiously, also in 1181, Henry II promulgated an Assize of Arms for his French territorial domains, but this prescribed different panoplies for the foot troops belonging to the second and third category. The soldiers of the second category were to have a helmet, hauberk of chainmail, spear and sword; the soldiers of the third category were to have a helmet, quilted aketon, spear and sword or bow and arrows. These differences are quite interesting, since they show two things: firstly, that most of the English commoners were too poor to own a sword, and secondly, that the longbow was not yet a popular alternative to the standard infantry spear. Henry III's Assize of 1242 modified the panoply required for each category of freemen:

Above left: Welsh warrior armed with sword. (Photo by Thomas Ortner and copyright to Armin Kaar)

Above right: Welsh warrior equipped with axe and round shield. (The Last Prince – O'Sullivan Beare and John Mullane)

members of the first were to have a helmet, hauberk of chainmail, spear, sword and knife; members of the second were to have a helmet, quilted aketon, spear, sword and knife; members of the third could have a bow and arrows, sword and knife or a single 'peasant weapon' (like a falchion or a gisarme). The most important innovation was the introduction of the bow as an alternative to the standard infantry weapons used by the third category.

Under Edward I, the nature of the English military forces changed considerably. First of all, knights and peasant infantrymen recruited according to the feudal system, rapidly became a decidedly secondary component of the English Army. They were replaced by professional soldiers who served for money and without limitations of time/space (something that had always hampered the expansionist campaigns of the previous Plantagenet kings). The familia regis of the monarch, had previously consisted of just a few knights acting as the personal bodyguard of the king; under Edward I, it was greatly expanded and came to comprise hundreds of knights and mounted sergeants who served for money and who responded only to the monarch. The royal household, in addition to the milites stipendiarii, started to include increasing numbers of mercenaries recruited from abroad (mostly from the remaining Plantagenet French possessions in Gascony). The great majority of the Gascon mercenaries were mounted crossbowmen, who moved on horse but fought on foot. The crossbow never became popular in England, due to the ascendancy of the longbow as the 'national weapon'; as a result, the crossbowmen of the English Plantagenet armies were all foreign mercenaries. Edward I, during his conquest of Wales, understood that the local longbowmen could have an enormous combat potential and thus soon started to recruit large numbers of them inside his military forces. Around 1285, almost two thirds of the infantrymen serving in the English Army were Welsh longbowmen, who had replaced the previous feudal infantry levies. Edward I also sponsored the adoption of the longbow as the standard weapon of the English commoners, since – in the future – he did not want to rely entirely on Welsh archers. The latter were usually organised in constabularies with 100 men each, like their English equivalents. The previous contingents of feudal infantry were usually organised in larger constabularies with 500 men each, but these had mostly disappeared by the beginning of Edward I's reign. A single constabulary with 100 infantrymen was usually divided into five sub-units with 20 soldiers each. Each constabulary was commanded by an officer – equipped as a mounted sergeant – who was known as 'centenar', while each sub-unit was commanded by a sort of non-comissioned officer – equipped as a foot sergeant – who was known as 'vintenar'.

The 1285 Statute of Winchester, which remained valid until the end of the period taken into account in this book, modified the panoply that each category of English soldier had to carry on the battlefield. It divided the English subjects who could be called to serve into six distinct categories, always formulated according to the economic capabilities of their members. The first category included individuals who owned more than £40 of land, who were required to equip themselves as heavy knights; the second category included individuals who owned more than £20 of land, who were required to equip themselves as mounted sergeants; the third category included individuals who owned more than £15 of land, who were required to equip themselves as heavy infantrymen with chainmail hauberk; the fourth category included individuals who owned more than £10 of land, who were required to equip themselves as medium infantrymen with a quilted aketon; the fifth category included individuals who owned more than £2 of land, who were required to equip themselves as longbowmen (with bow, sword and knife); and the sixth category included individuals who owned less than £2 of land, who could arm themselves with a longbow

Above left: Welsh warrior armed with axe. (The Last Prince – O'Sullivan Beare and John Mullane)

Above right: Welsh archer equipped with longbow. (The Last Prince – O'Sullivan Beare and John Mullane)

or with whatever 'peasant weapon' they might have. With the promulgation of the 'Statute of Winchester', the standard procedures for mobilisation were also changed. In case of war, the king was to appoint a 'Commission of Array', made up of experienced knights usually from the royal household; they were tasked with recruiting the needed number of soldiers from the various shires and urban centres of the realm and to assemble them into constabularies. Military service was performed at the individual's expense if conducted within the boundaries of his country, and at the king's expense if conducted outside the boundaries of the kingdom. During the early years of the XIV century, the Plantagenet monarchs started recruiting military contingents in a new way, according to the 'indenture system'. This worked quite simply: the monarch stipulated a formal contract with one of his nobles for raising a certain number of soldiers for a precise period of time in exchange for the payment of a pre-determined sum of money. The new system derived its name from the fact that such a contract had an indented edge that, in order to prevent forgery, had to match perfectly with the corresponding indents on the top or bottom edge of the king's counterfoil. The creation of the indenture system was the result of the feudal military organisation's gradual collapse; during the early Plantagenet period, the English barons were obliged to send their knights to the king in case of war, while by the beginning of the late Plantagenet period the monarch had to pay his nobles in exchange for their military services if they were mercenary warlords.

The Norman army that invaded England in 1066 included a sizeable number of mercenaries coming from northern France, and King William continued to recruit professional soldiers on the continent – from the French regions of Brittany, Anjou and Maine – for most of his reign. During the 'Anarchy' period, both King Stephen and Empress Matilda had sizeable mercenary contingents at their disposal. These mostly consisted of Welsh light infantrymen and Brabançon/Flemish heavy infantrymen. The latter were particularly appreciated, since they were the only foot soldiers of western Europe who could resist a cavalry charge on the open field thanks to their excellent personal equipment. A standard Brabançon/Flemish infantryman was a pikeman equipped with helmet and chainmail as well as with a shield. The pikes (known as geldons) of such professional soldiers, who were extremely loyal to their employers if paid regularly, were 10–12ft long and thus could cause serious harm to a heavy knight from a certain distance. Empress Matilda, who had ruled the Holy Roman Empire for several years, knew very well the excellent combat capabilities of the Brabançon/Flemish mercenary infantrymen, who continued to be employed in England by Henry II and Richard the Lionheart. The mercenary Welsh light infantrymen, equipped as fast-moving spearmen or as longbowmen, were mostly

Welsh archer in English service. (Confraternita del Leone)

employed by the early Plantagenets to fight in France. After the Battle of Bouvines and the signing of the Magna Charta, the number of foreign mercenaries employed by the English kings declined considerably since the powerful barons considered the contingents of professional soldiers as a potential threat to their freedom.

For their French military campaigns, however, the Plantagenet monarchs continued to recruit large numbers of local mercenaries (most notably Gascon crossbowmen). Since the English knights and feudal levies were always reluctant to serve overseas, the Plantagenet armies fighting in France mostly consisted of two categories of troops: local knights/feudal levies coming from the French regions that were under Plantagenet control, and mercenaries coming from various areas of France or from other regions, such as Wales or Flanders. After a portion of Ireland was occupied by the English, the Plantagenet military forces started to include some contingents of Irish 'auxiliaries'. These consisted of feudal levies that were

Above left: Scottish knight equipped for fighting on foot. (Photo by Thomas Ortner and copyright to Armin Kaar)

Above right: Scottish infantryman armed with spear. (Confraternita del Leone)

made up of light infantrymen, who were recruited by the Anglo-Irish lords who owned fiefdoms in the newly conquered areas of Ireland. Initially, the feudal contingents recruited by the Plantagenets in their French territorial possessions were of excellent quality and quite large, especially those coming from Normandy. These troops, however, could not be employed outside their home territories and usually refused to serve for long periods of time. They were organised and equipped very similarly to their English equivalents; it should be noted, however, that the French infantrymen in Plantagenet service included sizeable numbers of well-armed urban militiamen as well as well-trained crossbowmen. After most of the Plantagenet domains in France were lost during John Lackland's reign, only Gascony remained under English control. The military forces of the region included feudal contingents raised by the most prominent local nobles as well as urban militiamen coming from the major Gascony cities like Bordeaux.

During the Plantagenet period, the English Navy saw significant development, mostly because control of the English Channel was fundamental for connecting the Plantagenet domains in the British Isles with those located in France. The best warships of the medieval English Navy were provided to the Plantagenet monarchs by the famous Cinque Ports: Hastings, New Romney, Hythe, Dover and Sandwich. These were five coastal centres located on the English Channel that enjoyed a series of privileges in exchange for the military contribution that they gave to the Plantagenets. In 1155, a Royal Charter by Henry II established that the Cinque Ports had to maintain 57 vessels ready for royal service, for 15 days every year in times of peace and for longer periods in times of war. In exchange, the Cinque Ports enjoyed the following privileges: exemption from royal taxes, permission to levy tolls and permission to administer local justice in an autonomous way. Under John Lackland, the Cinque Ports became flourishing commercial centres and the main bases of the English Navy. Edward I, understanding the importance of these coastal settlements for his military plans, granted their citizens the right to bring goods into his kingdom without paying import duties. When a new war began, it was common practice for the royal authorities to supplement the warships provided by the Cinque Ports with impressed merchant vessels; the crews of these vessels were paid for their services and were mostly tasked with transporting military contingents. The owners of the impressed ships, however, received no compensation from the royal government. In addition to the above naval resources there was the small private fleet of the monarch, which was based at the Tower of London and near London Bridge. By 1330, these 'King's Ships' consisted of 40 vessels, which were used for patrol or escort duties.

The Norman milites were all protected by a hauberk or shirt of mail, which was made of several thousands of interlocking metal rings. The dimensions of each hauberk could vary considerably, since the sleeves could come only to the elbow or have full arm-length. The bottom part of a hauberk generally reached the knees but could be longer or shorter. Producing this kind of armour needed a long and costly process, which only nobles could sustain; in any case, the diffusion of the chainmail among knights was practically universal. By the last half of the 12th century, the personal protections of a knight also included some other elements made with mail, such as the 'chausses' (armour protecting the legs) and gloves. At that time, separate coifs of mail for protection of the head were not yet in use, and the portion of chainmail protecting head/neck was simply part of the hauberk. The chainmail was worn over a padded garment known as 'aketon', which offered additional protection to its wearer. The standard helmet of the Norman knights was the conical one with nasal, but a semi-spherical version of it having a full facial mask became increasingly common as time progressed. The skull of a nasal helmet could be raised from a single sheet of iron or be of composite construction. The nasal was fully integrated into either the skull or browband of the helmet; it was usually riveted to the skull or was part of a T-shaped piece protecting both the nose and the eyebrow. During the 12th century, the skull of the nasal helmets became more varied: it could have a forward-deflected apex (resembling the shape of a Phrygian cap) or it could be round-topped. The standard shield of the Norman milites was the so-called 'kite shield', which was specifically designed for cavalry use and gave a high degree of protection to its users. Kite-shaped, it was made of laminated wood and covered with stretched animal hide that could be painted to reproduce different decorative motifs. A band of metal was placed on the external edge of the shield for reinforcing it and – in correspondence with the handle – each kite shield had a round metal reinforcement on the front known as 'umbo', which could be pointed in order to be used

Above left: Scottish infantryman armed with axe. (Confraternita del Leone)

Above right: Scottish infantryman wearing padded defensive equipment. (Confraternita del Leone)

as an offensive weapon during close combat. Kite shields were usually equipped with 'enarmes' (leather gripping straps) on their back, which gripped them tightly to the arm even when their users relaxed their arms. They also had an additional long strap that enabled them to be slung over one shoulder when not in use. The standard dimensions of a kite shield corresponded to the approximate space placed between a horse's neck and its rider's thigh; the narrow bottom of the shield protected the rider's left leg and the pronounced upper curve protected both the left shoulder and the torso of the rider. Due to the peculiar features described above, the kite shield was perfect for cavalry use and was much more effective than the previous round shield.

The main offensive weapons of the Norman knights were the spear and the long sword. Norman spears were produced in two main versions: throwing spears and thrusting spears. The heads of the former had an average length of 20cm, while those of the latter had a standard length of 70cm. Spear heads consisted of two parts: the blade and the socket. The wooden shaft was fixed into the socket with one or two nails; sometimes spears could also have two projections on the side of the socket that were known as 'wings' and which were used to remove the spear from enemy shields more easily. Occasionally, the back end of the shaft was capped with a metal ferrule. Spear blades could be of two different kinds, the first of which was older than the second. The first model of blade was forged with a herringbone pattern along the middle and had curved edges, and it blended inconspicuously into the socket. The second model of blade had nearly straight edges (which ended in an angle at the base) and a marked narrowing as it merged into the socket. Wings were very common on the first model and quite rare on the second one. In addition to making extraction of the spear from enemy shields easier, wings could be used for hooking onto the edge of an enemy shield and creating an opening through which to strike. The wooden shaft of the thrusting spears was longer than that of the throwing spears; the former was 2.5/3m long, while the latter was 1.5m long. The diameter of all shafts was 2.5cm and sometimes narrowed towards the back end. Throwing spears were less popular than thrusting ones, since the Normans were the first knights in Feudal Europe to start using their thrusting spears tucked under the armpit during frontal charges. Thanks to the employment of the stirrups and of solid saddles having tall pommels, the Norman milites could remain stable on their horses while thrusting with the spears placed under their armpits. Before the widespread adoption of the stirrups, the cavalry contingents of Antiquity wielded their spears overarm and thus could not employ them for thrusting with great power. Swords were much more expensive and complex to produce than spears. The Norman sword was a single-handed weapon that was designed to leave one of the warrior's hands free in order to hold the shield. The hilt consisted of three parts: back-hilt, grip and fore-hilt. Sometimes the fore-hilt was made up of two parts, the hindmost one of which was commonly known as the pommel. Most of the hilts were made of iron, but sometimes they could be obtained from bronze. The total length of a Norman sword was of 90–95cm, while the average length of the blade was of 75–80cm. Blades were 5–6cm wide, and their weight was restricted towards the point; this was obtained by tapering the single blades both in breadth and in thickness towards the point. As a result of the above, blade thickness was 6mm near the hilt and 2mm at the point of the sword. To reduce the weight further and to increase flexibility, a groove was forged and ground out along the middle of the blade. The centre of gravity of the weapon was near the hilt and this made it quite easy to handle. Many swords, especially those belonging to the richest individuals, had decorative inscriptions on the blade and decorated hilts. All swords were carried in leather-bound wooden scabbards that were often suspended from a strap across the right shoulder. Like the scabbard, the hilt was made of an organic material like horn or antler.

During the last decades of the 12th century, due to the increasing diffusion of the crossbow on the European fields of battle, most of the knights started to abandon their previous helmets with no protection for the face (except for the nasal) and replace them with new ones with different patterns of facial masks. The latter were fixed and initially gave protection only to the frontal part of the face; with the progression of time, however, they started to have bigger dimensions in order to also cover the sides of the face. As a result of this process, the helmets gradually transformed themselves into full 'great helms', providing complete protection to the head. Regarding shields, there was a progressive transition from the Norman kite shield to the new 'triangular shield' that was used for most of the Middle Ages. The adoption of closed helmets stopped any possibility of recognising the identity of the knight on the field of battle; to solve this problem, heraldry saw a rapid growth and each noble family started to develop a distinctive emblem. This was initially painted only on the shield of each knight, but it was later reproduced also on a new piece of garment that came into use: the 'surcoat'. The surcoat was worn over the hauberk and initially had no embroidered decorations. In the following decades, the heraldic display of each knight was completed by the presence of a coloured crest that was placed on top of the helmet.

Until 1200, war horses were not protected with any specific piece of equipment; during the early decades of the 12th century,

Highland Scottish warrior armed with sword. (Photo by Thomas Ortner and copyright to Armin Kaar)

however, the large diffusion of the crossbow led to the creation of new defensive elements specifically designed for horses. Initially, these protected only the head, but were later improved in order to protect the entire body of the horse; they could be made with quilted material or with chainmail. The second half of the 12th century saw the development of plate armour, which started to be worn in combination with the traditional hauberks. This important evolution, like several others, was encouraged by the increasing diffusion and effectiveness of the crossbow. Initially plate armour was mostly made of 'cuir bouilli' (boiled leather) and consisted of disks protecting the shoulders and the knees. Very soon, however, leather started to be substituted with metal and new pieces of plate armour – like greaves – came into use. The protection of the head/neck, meanwhile, had been improved thanks to the introduction of a hood made of chainmail – known as 'camail' – which was separated from the hauberk. The torso of the milites started to be protected by a robust coat-of-plates, formed by many small and flat pieces of iron that were all riveted together inside a thick fabric garment (buckled at the back). During this same period, most of the knights began using a mace or axe as an alternative 'secondary weapon' to the long sword. By the beginning of the 14th century, the hauberk of each knight was usually supplemented by a series of additional defensive elements of plate armour, which could be richly decorated: 'vambraces', 'cuisses', 'gauntlets', 'poleyns' and 'sabatons'. Meanwhile, a new form of open helmet, known as 'chapel de fer', had become quite popular

Above left: Highland Scottish warrior. (Photo by Thomas Ortner and copyright to Armin Kaar)

Above right: Irish 'galloglass' (foreign warriors) wearing camail and helmet. (Photo by Thomas Ortner and copyright to Armin Kaar)

also among the milites. This wide-brimmed helmet was initially designed for the infantry, but since it was much more comfortable to wear than the various models of 'great helm', the chapel de fer was also adopted by knights. Sergeants were equipped more or less like the knights, but their armour was usually lighter than that of the milites; the milites adopted plate armour, for example, while most of the sergeants continued to wear simple hauberks.

The poorest feudal infantrymen had no military equipment to speak of: they went to war with their ordinary clothes and were mostly armed with their agricultural tools. The luckiest of them had a padded aketon and a simple helmet (usually of a conical shape). The foot sergeants and the mercenary infantrymen coming from the continent were much better equipped than the peasant levies: they all had helmets and frequently wore a full chainmail over their aketon. Some of them even had chausses, while almost all were armed with long pikes that had to be used with both hands. The quilted aketon – the armour of the poor – was quite popular also among the archers who were part of the feudal infantry. It was usually made of linen or wool, with the stuffing being obtained from different materials like scrap cloth or horse hair. Quilted hoods for protection of the head were usually worn together with the aketon, which was improved during the 13th century with the addition of some new components like quilted collars or quilted gloves. Some of the feudal infantrymen did not have a shield, while the mercenary foot soldiers were usually equipped with kite or triangular shields. The archers usually carried a sword and a knife in addition to the longbow; sometimes they could also have a small round shield; they wore no armour and had a light aketon. Crossbowmen often had hauberks or aketons, worn together with a chapel de fer; since their main weapon had to be used with both hands, they had no shields and thus were usually deployed behind a line of 'pavisiers' – specialised infantrymen equipped with a large and flat shield known as 'pavise'. The pavise became popular in England only during the Hundred Years' War. The archers of the Norman period were equipped with bows made from yew, ash or elm; these had a draw force of 100lb and an effective range of 200m. From a technical point of view, they were 'longbows', since they were obtained from a single piece of wood. The overall height of a Norman bow generally corresponded to that of its user. When not in use, a Norman bow was almost straight; when strung, it was nearly D-shaped in cross-section. Arrowheads could be of three different kinds: blade-shaped, spike-shaped and chisel-shaped. The second model was that specifically designed for combat use, since the other two were employed also for hunting. Each arrowhead was fixed with a tang to its shaft, which was made of wood, had feathers applied on the back and was 65–75cm long.

Wales

At the beginning of the 11th century the territory of present-day Wales was fragmented into a series of small princedoms, which were constantly at war against each other. These petty states were the direct heirs of some extremely old tribal traditions, which had changed very little during the long centuries of Saxon dominance over England. Despite being politically fragmented, the Welsh had been able to preserve their freedom for a long time by repulsing all the Saxon attacks directed against their lands; they had become famous for their warlike 'national' spirit and were with out doubt an extremely dangerous enemy for any army that attempted to invade. From a geographical point of view, Wales is characterised by very harsh terrain that is not suitable for battlefield use by large cavalry contingents. The only troop type that could fight in Wales with a high degree of effectiveness was light infantry; for this reason, the great majority of the Welsh warriors were equipped as highly mobile skirmishers. Those coming from northern Wales were mostly equipped as spearmen, while those coming from southern Wales were armed with the deadly longbow. The latter was the 'national' weapon of Wales during the medieval period and – as we have already seen – it was progressively adopted by an increasing number of English foot soldiers as their main weapon. Around 1100, the various princedoms of Wales were subdivided into a series of minor territorial entities, having a tribal nature and being known as 'cantrefs'; each of the cantrefs was dominated by a minor 'uchelwr' (warlord). All the able-bodied Welsh males over 14 years of age were expected to serve under their warlord in time of war; according to Giraldus Cambrensis' (c.1146–c.1223) *Description of Wales* (c.1193), all the Welsh freemen were extremely happy to fight for the defence of their homeland or to raid the territories of their local enemies. Military service was more a right than a duty and the endemic 'state of war' existing in medieval Wales had greatly improved the combat capabilities of the local warriors. They knew their home territories very well and were used to fighting with 'hit-and-run' guerrilla tactics that based their success on high mobility. The Welsh warriors received no pay for their military service, but could divide among themselves the booty taken from defeated enemies. They were quite reluctant to fight for long periods of time outside the borders of their princedom and thus 'external campaigns' usually lasted for a maximum of six weeks. Any

Irish galloglass equipped with 'sparth' axe and sword. (Photo by Thomas Ortner and copyright to Armin Kaar)

freeman incapable of attending military service had to equip and send another individual in his place. Unfree males were usually conscripted only to perform auxiliary duties like building encampments or transporting materials.

Each Welsh major prince had a retinue of professional soldiers under his command; these were collectively known as 'teulu' or 'family'. Very often they were relatives of the warlord prince, who were given sustenance and land by the prince in exchange for their military service. Members of the teulu were the only Welsh warriors to have horses, but they usually dismounted to fight and thus did not perform as 'true' cavalry. In most cases, the military family of a major prince numbered around 120 professional warriors, who were all uchelwyr (the plural for uchelwr). They were equipped with helmet and chainmail that was quite similar to the contemporary English knights, while the Welsh commoners fighting as spearmen or archers wore no personal protections and carried only their offensive weapons in combat. Welsh spears were not particularly long, since on most occasions they were used as throwing javelins. Welsh shields were round, and they were carried by all the uchelwyr and by some of the spearmen. Sometimes a Welsh prince could enlarge his teulu by recruiting foreign mercenaries; these, on most occasions, were Irishmen or warriors of the Viking communities still existing in Ireland (mostly coming from Dublin). The Norman kings of England, having been unable to conquer Wales, created a series of highly autonomous baronies on the border that divided the Welsh lands from the English ones. These baronies, known as 'Welsh Marches', were assigned to the most warlike Norman nobles who were tasked with defending the frontier as well as with penetrating – slowly but steadily – into Welsh lands. The barons of the Welsh Marches continued to be the most powerful warlords of England also under the Plantagenets, since they enjoyed a series of military privileges: they, for example, could build castles and mobilise troops without asking for the formal permission of the monarch. The military forces of the 'Marcher Lords' were made up of the most battle-hardened veterans of England and played a prominent role during the early campaigns that were fought by the Plantagenets in Ireland. They included large numbers of Welsh longbowmen since the last decades of the 11th century, something that made them quite different from the military contingents of the other English barons. Two of the most prominent Marcher Lords, Gilbert de Clare and his son Richard, were nicknamed 'Strongbow' probably because their military successes were based on a substantial use of Welsh longbowmen.

Scotland

By the time of the Norman conquest of England, the territory of Scotland had already been unified as the 'Kingdom of Alba', which assumed the denomination of 'Kingdom of Scotland' only after the outbreak of the Scottish Independence Wars caused by the dynastic crisis of 1286. In medieval Scotland all able-bodied males aged 16–60 could be called to serve in the 'exercitus Scoticanus' or 'common army', which included freemen (most of whom were farmers owning small landed properties) as well as 'neyfs' or 'unfree men'. The latter were not slaves, but individuals who were tied for life to the land where they had been born. The neyfs could be sold or given away with the land on which they lived and worked but were not treated as slaves. The Scottish territory was divided into small units of arable land – known as 'arachors' – for which inhabitants were usually asked to provide one soldier each in case of mobilisation. When needed every free or unfree man owning a cow could be recruited. In each Scottish shire, the infantrymen who made up the exercitus Scoticanus were raised by local officials known as 'thanes'. The contingents of the various thanes were then grouped at the orders of a major chieftain. This kind of traditional Gaelic military organisation, which comprised no cavalry contingents, remained unchanged for centuries since the process that saw the introduction of feudalism into Scotland was extremely slow. By the end of the 13th century, the Gaelic chieftains of the Lowlands had mostly been transformed

Irish 'kerns' (Irish light infantrymen) from the late 14th century; one is armed with sword, the other with sparth axe. (The Last Prince – O'Sullivan Beare and John Mullane)

into feudal earls by the monarchs of Scotland, while in the Highlands feudalism was still practically non-existent. The Scottish kings tried to have military households consisting of mercenary English knights, since the latter had no rivals in Scotland from a tactical point of view; the Scottish nobles, however, always stopped their monarchs' plans by revolting against them when they recruited too many foreign mercenaries. After the Battle of Stirling Bridge William Wallace tried to introduce some form of 'conscription' by inflicting heavy punishments on those individuals who failed to answer the call to arms, but his innovations were soon abandoned after his death. According to a 'Statute of Arms' promulgated in 1318, every Scottish layman possessing at least £10 in goods was to serve by equipping himself with helmet and padded aketon; laymen possessing less than £10 in goods, were to equip themselves just with a spear or with a bow. Once each year, the personal panoply of each potential soldier had to be inspected by royal officials.

Irish kern wearing leather cap. (Photo by Thomas Ortner and copyright to Armin Kaar)

The few Scottish feudal knights serving during the period taken into account were equipped exactly like their English equivalents; the infantrymen of the 'common army', instead, were mostly armed as pikemen. They wore short-sleeved hauberks of chainmail or padded aketons, which were employed together with a simple 'skull helmet' or – since the early 14th century – a chapel de fer. These were usually worn over a padded hood or 'infula', but there were several foot soldiers who used the infula as their only head protection since they were not rich enough to purchase a helmet. The pikes had wooden shafts up to 15ft long and had to be handled with both hands; as a result, the Scottish foot soldiers could carry only small round shields made of wooden planks (sometimes reinforced with metal bosses). These were of some use only against enemy arrows coming from a long distance. As a secondary weapon a Scottish infantryman could carry a small axe or a knife. The Scottish pikemen fought in a compact tactical formation known as a schiltron, which was an evolution of the previous – and extremely common – 'shield wall'. A schiltron was a phalanx-style battle formation, the main aim of which was to present an enemy cavalry charge with a defensive perimeter that the horses would refuse to breach. William Wallace perfected the schiltron formation but did not invent it, since the use of this tactical deployment is attested in Scotland already in the 11th century. The schiltrons could be of two alternative kinds: circular and rectilinear. The first was essentially static: the soldiers in the front ranks knelt with their pike butts fixed into the ground, while those in the rear ranks levelled their pikes over their comrades' heads. The result was a thick-set grove of pikes, which could be fortified by driving stakes into the ground before the men of the front tanks; the stakes could be linked with ropes. The rectilinear schiltron was capable of conducting offensive actions and was greatly developed by Robert the Bruce, who drilled his men in the use of the pike as an offensive anti-cavalry weapon. For an infantry army like the exercitus Scoticanus, employing the schiltrons was the only way to defeat the numerous and effective heavy cavalry of the Plantagenets.

Ireland

Medieval Ireland consisted of several small kingdoms, each of which was based on tribal units singularly known as 'tuath' and consisting of several family groups who had lived in the same territory for a long time. The various family groups could be free ones (the 'soer-chele') or unfree ones (the 'doer-chele'). The first were dominant inside their tuath, while the second had to accept the decisions taken by the members of the soer-chele, more or less like vassals. The leading nobles of the soer-chele could be kings of three different types: 'Ri-tuaithe', king of one tuath; 'Rui-ri', king of more than one tuath; 'Ri-ruirech', monarch of one of the Irish kingdoms. In addition to the above, there were also the so-called 'High Kings', monarchs of one kingdom who temporarily came to exert a direct or indirect influence over some of the other Irish realms. The title of 'High King' was mostly a ceremonial one, since during the medieval period – with the notable exception of Brian Boru (c.941–23 April 1014) – no Irish king was able to unify the whole island under his control or to stop the continuous inter-state wars that ravaged Ireland. In case of war, all the able-bodied adult males of both the soer-chele and doer-chele were to follow their Ri-tuaithe or Rui-ri in battle; the latter, of course, was obliged to serve under his Ri-ruirech when required to do so. At the beginning of the 11th century, the military forces fielded by a single tuath usually consisted of 700 warriors, who were assembled into a 'buiden' or 'band'. Each buiden consisted of seven 'hundreds' or 'cets'. With the progression of time, most of the Irish military units started to consist of 300, rather than 700, warriors and were known as 'tricha cet'. There were no precise time limits for military service, but in most cases, it was impossible for a king to raise his military forces during autumn or spring because in those periods of the year his subjects had to work in the fields. The Viking invasions and incursions changed Ireland forever when the Scandinavian presence on the island became a permanent one. From the encounter between the Irish and the Vikings a new mixed population emerged, that of the 'Gall-Gael' or 'Foreign Gaels'. They soon earned a solid reputation as skilled warriors and started to be employed as mercenaries by the various Irish warlords. Before the arrival of the Scandinavians, the few foreign mercenaries hired by the Irish kings came from Scotland; with the progression of time, however, consistent numbers of Gall-Gael professional soldiers started to act as the 'household' of various Irish monarchs.

After the late 11th century, some elements of the military system described above started to change. The old buiden of 700 warriors was gradually replaced by the new 'cat mor' of 1,000 warriors as the new basic military unit; the cat mor, however, continued to consist of 'hundreds' or cet. By the time of the Plantagenet invasion, the tricha cet had transformed itself into an administrative unit, with each tuath consisting of three 'bailles' (groups) of 100 households. In case of war, each household was to provide one warrior, but general mobilisations could see a single household providing two or three men for military service. The traditional Irish military system began declining after the Plantagenet invasion, as the tribal contingents were usually reluctant to serve far from their homes for long periods of service. The traditional system had been created to conduct rapid inter-tribal campaigns, not long wars fought against foreign invaders who had settled a portion of Ireland in a permanent way. The crisis of the traditional military system corresponded to the increase in importance of the foreign mercenaries of mixed Irish-Scandinavian descent, and the Irish monarchs started to recruit larger numbers of professional soldiers from the Gall-Gael communities living in Ireland. Urban centres that were still inhabited by large Scandinavian

Irish kern. Note the excellent manufacture of his costume, which includes a 'lonar' (short jacket) worn over a 'leine' (long tunic). (The Last Prince – O'Sullivan Beare and John Mullane)

groups – like Wexford and Waterford as well as Dublin – became the main bases of these mercenaries who fought like Vikings and who were known as 'Ostmen'. Ruled by hereditary earls, the Ostmen earned a living fighting as mercenaries or raiding the British Isles as pirates on their agile warships characterised by their distinctive Scandinavian design. By the end of the 12th century, however, most of the Irish urban centres inhabited by Gall-Gael communities had been occupied by the Plantagenets and thus the Irish kings had to look elsewhere to find new contingents of mercenaries. The Western Isles (the Hebrides and the Isle of Man) as well as the western seaboard of Scotland, were still inhabited by large Norse-Gael communities, which were the result of the encounter between the local population and the Vikings that had taken place several decades before. The warriors of these mixed communities, like the Irish Gall-Gael, fought in the Viking way and were well known for their combat ferocity. Around 1150, they started to be recruited as mercenaries by the Irish kings, initiating a practice that would have lasted until the early 17th century.

By 1250, they had started to be called 'galloglass' (foreign warriors) and had become a permanent component of each Irish monarch's personal household. Since the early 14th century, the Norse-Scottish mercenaries were considered to be a real 'elite' inside Irish armies, because they were better trained and better equipped than the ordinary Irish tribal warriors. The galloglass were organised into 'corughadhs' or 'companies' with 100–160 men, and each of them had a senior servant who performed auxiliary duties (like transporting the personal equipment of the warrior) as well as a junior servant who cooked. The basic unit formed by one warrior, one senior servant and one junior servant was known as a 'spar'. The term spar derived from the word 'sparth', which was used to indicate the deadly double-handed axe carried by each galloglass. With the ascendancy of the galloglass, the standard Irish light infantrymen with 'tribal' organisation started to be known as 'kerns'. In 1307, the Statute of Winchester was applied on the Irish territories of the Plantagenets; as a result, the Anglo-Irish feudal lords could recruit the able-bodied Irish males living on their fiefdoms in case of war. It should be noted, however, that most of the Anglo-Irish troops fighting for the Plantagenets consisted of a few English knights who had settled in Ireland and larger numbers of kerns provided by the Irish warlords who were subjects or allies of the English. The standard Irish medieval warrior, before the appearance of the galloglass, was a light infantryman armed with one short spear and two throwing javelins. Small round shields were quite popular, but, in contrast, helmets were

Irish kern. The Ionar was usually decorated with rich embroidery of natural elements, like the one shown here. (The Last Prince – O'Sullivan Beare and John Mullane)

rare; armour was non-existent. Only the noble warriors used chainmail and went to the battlefield mounted on horses. All the Irish fighters had a long dagger for close combat, called a 'skein'. Until the first half of the 13th century, the Irish warriors did not employ bows but only slings; later, some of them started to arm themselves as archers, but with short bows of a local design and not with the much more effective Welsh longbow. In addition to the few mounted nobles, the small Irish cavalry contingents comprised some light horsemen armed with throwing javelins. According to Giraldus Cambrensis' precious descriptions, the galloglasses were equipped as heavy infantrymen with a helmet and hauberk of chainmail.

Above left: Irish archer wearing leather cap. (Photo by Thomas Ortner and copyright to Armin Kaar)

Above right: Irish archer equipped with longbow and sword. (Photo by Thomas Ortner and copyright to Armin Kaar)

Bibliography

Ambler, S.T., *The Song of Simon de Montfort: England's First Revolutionary and the Death of Chivalry*, Picador, 2019.

Asbridge, T., *The Greatest Knight: The remarkable life of William Marshal, the Power behind five English Thrones*, Simon & Schuster, 2015.

Barber, R., *Henry II. A Prince amongst Princes*, Penguin, 2015.

Barratt, N., *The Restless Kings: Henry II, his Sons and the Wars for the Plantagenet Crown*, Faber & Faber, 2019.

Bartlett, C., *English Longbowman 1330-1515*, Osprey Publishing, 1995.

Bartlett, R., *England under the Norman and Angevin Kings 1075-1225*, Oxford University Press, 2003.

Bartlett, W.B., *Richard the Lionheart: the Crusader King of England*, Amberley Publishing, 2019.

Cannan, F., *Galloglass 1250-1600*, Osprey Publishing, 2010.

Gravett, C., *English Medieval Knight 1200-1300*, Osprey Publishing, 2002.

Gravett, C., *Norman Knight 950-1204*, Osprey Publishing, 1994.

Green, J.A., *Henry I: King of England and Duke of Normandy*, Cambridge University Press, 2009.

Heath, I., *Armies of Feudal Europe 1066-1300*, Wargames Research Group, 1989.

Heath, I., *Armies of the Dark Ages 600-1066*, Wargames Research Group, 1980.

Jones, D., *The Plantagenets: The Warrior Kings and Queens who made England*, Viking, 2013.

Loades, M., *The Longbow*, Osprey Publishing, 2013.

Morris, M., *A Great and Terrible King: Edward I and the forging of Britain*, Pegasus, 2017.

Morris, M., *King John: Treachery, Tyranny and the Road to Magna Carta*, Hutchinson, 2015.

Nicolle, D., *French Medieval Armies 1000-1300*, Osprey Publishing, 1991.

Nicolle, D., *The Normans*, Osprey Publishing, 1987.

Prestwich, M., *Plantagenet England 1225-1360*, Oxford University Press, 2007.

Rothero, C., *The Scottish and Welsh Wars 1250-1400*, Osprey Publishing, 1984.

Spencer, C., *The White Ship: Conquest, Anarchy and the Wrecking of Henry I's Dream*, William Collins, 2020.

Weir, A., *Eleanor of Aquitaine: By the Wrath of God, Queen of England*, Vintage, 2008.

Wise, T., *Saxon, Viking and Norman*, Osprey Publishing, 1979.

The Re-enactors who Contributed to this Book

Historia Aquitanorum

Historia Aquitanorum is a French living history association, which re-enacts both the civilian and military daily life of the second half of the 12th century, in a seigniory (the position, authority, or domain of a feudal lord) located in the Dukedom of Aquitaine. Our main goal is to be as historically accurate as possible and help people discover this little-known period. All of our diverse achievements come from serious research done in various domains, such as iconography (i.e., illuminations, sculptures and frescoes), texts (i.e., cartularies, literary sources) and archaeological sources. We make people aware of this period through true-to-life historical characters and thematic workshops during medieval celebrations or historical recreation and have taken part in film shoots and TV programmes. We also organise the gatherings of various troops similar to ours from all over France and even abroad (Battle of Malemort, L'Epée et le Bourdon). You can easily contact us to check our availabilities and decide what we can offer for your project. Send us an email, we would be pleased to share our knowledge and our passion.

Contacts:
E-mail: info@historia-aquitanorum.fr
Website: www.historia-aquitanorum.fr
Facebook: https://www.facebook.com/Historia-Aquitanorum-644585265732379/

De Gueules et d'Argent

De Gueules et d'Argent is a living history group based in France. It seeks to re-enact the troop of 'chatelaines' (French feudal lords tasked with defending a castle) living in the county of Savoy at the pivotal time of the end of the 12th century and the beginning of the 13th century. This group also practises historical European martial arts, the practice of feudal individual (duels) and group combat. Nathanaël Dos Reis, leader of the group, is a historian preparing a PhD thesis on the evolution of the military equipment of the equestrian fighter from the 11th to the 13th century.

Contacts:
E-mail: degueulesetdargent@gmail.com and nathanaeldosreis.culture@gmail.com
Facebook: https://www.facebook.com/degueulesetdargent

Milites Pagenses

Milites Pagenses is a small Breton association of historical re-enactment working on the first decades of the 12th century. The focus of our work is the evocation of the household of a knight and of peasant feudal levies from this historical period.

Contacts:
Website: https://militespagenses.jimdofree.com/
Facebook: https://www.facebook.com/MilitesPagenses

Les Guerriers du Moyen-Age

The Les Guerriers du Moyen-Age association is a French historical reconstruction association created in 2001. The associative project focuses on civil and military life from the end of the 12th century to the end of the 13th century. Regarding the 12th century, the project focuses on the hospital of Saint Jean de Jerusalem. Concerning the 13th century, the association recreates a bourgeois militia of 1274, organised and ruled in Saint-Maur-des-Fossés (near Paris). Our association also includes a section of historical European martial arts focused on military combat on foot from the 13th century to the beginning of the 14th century.

Contacts:
Email: gma@guerriersma.com
Website: www.guerriersma.com
Facebook: https://www.facebook.com/GMA.reconstitution/

Les Seigneurs d'Orient

Les Seigneurs d'Orient (The Lords of the Orient) is an historical re-enactment club based in Menton (France) since 2017. Our 30-person club is made up mainly of history students and teachers. Our area of expertise is the 12th century Near East and especially the Oriental Latin States (Outre Mer/Holy Land). We re-enact both Jerusalem's king court and a Syrian Emir court, including camp, furniture, civil and military outfits, and also run workshops. We cover projects from the First Crusade to the 13th century. The Lords of the Orient is part of the Living History Lovers Federation with The Somatophylakes, re-enacting Greeks and Macedonian phalanxes. We are therefore able to gather more than 40 fully equipped adults in a large camp. We take part in historical festivals, patrimonial exhibitions and run conferences on feudal society and 12th century Oriental Latin States. We've been hired for television documentaries by Patrick Spica Productions – *RMC Découverte (The secret of Monaco's Grimaldi fortress)* – and ZED production – *Curiosity (The siege of Acre)* – and for books or magazine publishers such as Pen & Sword Books and Éditions Heimdal. Our main activities include: historical research, artefact fabrication, civil and military outfit building, sword-shield and lance-shield medieval fighting, military group movements and formations, camp life and shows.

Contacts:
E-mail: cyril.errera@hotmail.com
Website: https://lesseigneursdorient.wixsite.com/lesite
Facebook: https://www.facebook.com/Lesseigneursdorient/

Sericum et ferrum

We are a re-enactment group focusing on Anglo-Norman lesser nobility in the time between 1180 and 1200. We try to reconstruct everything, from clothes to armour, as best we can and always try to get better at what we are doing. Analysing historical sources and reading are the most important parts of our hobby, so we support authors however we can. Our goal is to teach history in a different and exciting way to everyone who is interested. We are located near Bremen in Germany and co-operate worldwide.

Contact:
Facebook: https://www.facebook.com/Sericumetferrum

Armin Kaar

Mag Armin Kaar studied Celtic Studies at the University of Vienna with a focus on medieval Welsh literature. He also served as historical advisor for the Swiss band Eluveitie for their album *Helvetios* about the Gallic Wars and published several articles for the German hobby magazine *LARP-Zeit*. He has created costumes for re-enactment and fantasy groups since 15 years of age as a hobby. Among the several periods he re-enacts, his special interests are 16th century Britain, the Thirty Years' War and the English Civil War. His current project concerns Ukrainian Zaporozhian Cossacks. You can find his creations and photos via Instagram (@mimins_workshop).

Contact:
Facebook: https://www.facebook.com/profile.php?id=100022837253065

The Last Prince – O'Sullivan Beare

The Last Prince – O'Sullivan Beare, is a project founded by Conchobhar Ó Súilleabháin. It tells the epic story of the 1603 march of O'Sullivan Beare. This was when, after the famous Battle of Kinsale and the ferocious clash of two cultures, in a fight for survival, 1,000 native Gaels of Ireland fled their homes in the hope of freedom 300 miles away. In the middle of a cruel winter, 600 civilians, with only 400 soldiers to protect them, crossed a land ravaged by war, famine and treachery. They fought near-constant battles for the next 14 days, until finally reaching their destination with only 35 people remaining. Bravely led each and every step of the way by 'The Last Prince', Donal Cam O'Sullivan Beare, this is an epic story of endurance, hope, cruelty, victory and the indomitable spirit of the Gael. Our team tells this story through a style of storytelling that involves the use of educational living history displays and re-enactments on the hallowed ground and in the very footsteps of those who endured all those years ago in 1603.

Contacts:
Website: www.thelastprince.ie
Facebook: https://www.facebook.com/profile.php?id=100063653335641

Other books you might like:

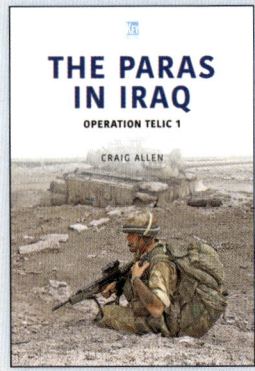

Modern Wars Series, Vol. 1

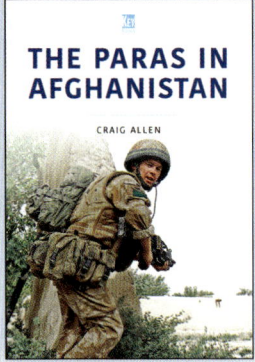

Modern Wars Series, Vol. 2

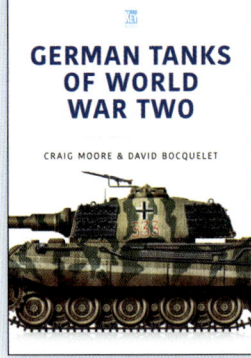

Military Vehicles and Artillery Series, Vol. 1

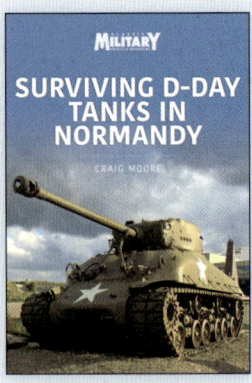

Military Vehicles and Artillery Series, Vol. 2

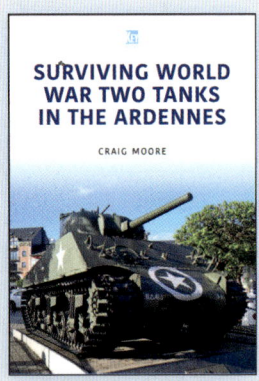

Military Vehicles and Artillery Series, Vol. 4

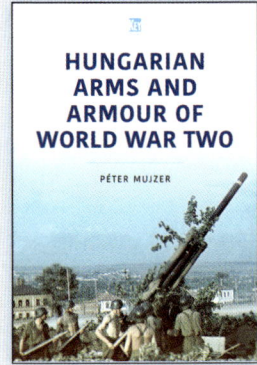

Military Vehicles and Artillery Series, Vol. 5

For our full range of titles please visit:
shop.keypublishing.com/books

VIP Book Club

Sign up today and receive
TWO FREE E-BOOKS

Be the first to find out about our forthcoming book releases and receive exclusive offers.

Register now at **keypublishing.com/vip-book-club**

Our VIP Book Club is a 100% spam-free zone, and we will never share your email with anyone else. You can read our full privacy policy at: privacy.keypublishing.com